W9-BNT-095

Solomon and Teagno have done an exquisite job bringing hope into darkness. They provide the education, skills and rationale for staying the course when everything seems bleak. Allow them to lead you in overcoming betrayal and reconnecting with the one you love.

> —Ellyn Bader, Ph.D., codirector of the Couples Institute and author of *Tell Me No Lies*

Intimacy After Infidelity is loaded with practical exercises and concrete advice that will help partners construct a strong and resilient relationship after an affair. Couples struggling with issues of trust and forgiveness will find it immediately useful.

> —Janis Abrahms Spring, Ph.D., author of *After the Affair* and *How Can I Forgive You?*

Intimacy After Infidelity is clear, informative, challenging, and smart—and most of all a tremendous source of hope for all couples who have endured the trauma of infidelity. The authors interweave sound theory, clinical stories, and structured exercises to help couples understand what the hell went wrong and why. And they give couples tools to pick up the pieces and (if they can commit to maturely facing the fear, loneliness, and anger) put this relationship back together again actually better and more truly intimate than ever before. I highly recommend this book!

> —David B. Wexler, Ph.D., author of *When Good Men Behave Badly* and *Is He Depressed or What?*, and executive director of the Relationship Training Institute

For those courageous souls who wish to repair, rebuild, and rejoin after an infidelity, this wonderfully wise guide can be a gift to your emerging new relationship. Developing new skills and knowledge is essential when you travel over emotionally painful terrain. This book is a trusty companion for your journey.

—Peter Pearson, Ph.D., cofounder of the
Couples Institute in Menlo Park, CA

A must read for everyone going through the pain of infidelity as well as for everyone who wants to improve his or her marriage —full of sound, practical advice on how to improve your marriage no matter what the obstacles.

—Cloé Madanes, president of the
Robbins-Madanes Center for
Strategic Intervention

intimacy
after infidelity

HOW TO
REBUILD & AFFAIR-PROOF
YOUR MARRIAGE

STEVEN D. SOLOMON, PH.D.
LORIE J. TEAGNO, PH.D.

New Harbinger Publications, Inc.

Distributed in Canada by Raincoast Books

Copyright © 2006 by Steven Solomon and Lorie Teagno
New Harbinger Publications, Inc.
5674 Shattuck Avenue
Oakland, CA 94609
www.newharbinger.com

Cover design by Amy Shoup; Text design by Michele Waters-Kermes; Acquired by Catharine Sutker

---

Library of Congress Cataloging-in-Publication Data

Solomon, Steven D.
  Intimacy after infidelity : how to rebuild and affair-proof your marriage / Steven D. Solomon and Lorie J. Teagno.
      p. cm.
  ISBN-13: 978-1-57224-461-0
  ISBN-10: 1-57224-461-5
  1. Adultery. 2. Marriage. 3. Man-woman relationships. I. Teagno, Lorie J. II. Title.

HQ806.S29 2006
306.73'6—dc22

                            2006024435

09 08 07

10 9 8 7 6 5 4 3 2

To our wonderful spouses,
Esther and Mike

contents

acknowledgments

We want to express our deep gratitude to Ellyn Bader and Peter Pearson for teaching us so much about helping couples. They are wonderful models of truly gifted couples therapists. They lit the way for us and for that we will always be thankful.

From the moment she heard us give a presentation on infidelity at a California Psychological Association convention, Catharine Sutker at New Harbinger Publications has been so helpful and supportive to us. This book is in large part a product of her encouragement and guidance. We also want to thank Holly Taines White and Carole Honeychurch, whose editing skills made such a difference in polishing the finished product.

We would be remiss not to thank the hundreds of clients who have shared their emotional and relationship lives with us and trusted us to help them find their paths. Our work with them has been mutually beneficial: while we have been privileged to show them new ways to love and be loved, their strength and resilience have enriched us and they have taught us the value of emotional intimacy in all relationships.

We also want to express our appreciation for the encouragement, understanding, and love we have received from our fantastic children, Lewis, Amy, Gracie, Adam, and Aaron. Not only were they patient during the many hours we spent immersed in writing, but each in their own way has taught us so much about love, commitment, and mutual relationship work.

Most importantly, we both know that this book would never have been written were it not for the love and support of our wonderful spouses, Esther and Mike. They have taught us so much about intimacy, about the strength that comes from love, and about the ongoing work that enables Long-Term Love Relationships to flourish.

We are truly blessed to have had so many people help us grow and learn about love and intimacy. This book is an effort to share these lessons with others.

/introduction

the shock of discovery

*Courage is the price that life exacts for
granting peace.* —Amelia Earhart

We're so, so sorry.

It's excruciating. The one person in the world whom you placed your trust in above all others, the one person in the world whose love you relied on, has horribly betrayed your trust and love.

There are very few things in life that are as painful as what you are experiencing right now. If you have recently discovered the infidelity, if you just learned the depth and extent of your partner's betrayal(s), you are likely undergoing the agony of a broken heart. If you're like most people, right now you're probably having some of these feelings: at times your chest hurts, you feel sick to your stomach, you can't eat, and you have trouble sleeping. You can't stop having these horrible thoughts of him with another woman, images that are knives in your heart. Maybe you're filled with white-hot rage. Or you may simply have picked up this book to determine if leaving the relationship after his betrayal is the right decision for you.

However you're experiencing the pain of your partner's betrayal, one of the worst things is that not only is your relationship shattered, if not destroyed, but his unfaithfulness also damages how you feel about yourself. You start questioning your worth and attractiveness, doubting your ability to wisely choose a partner, and wondering whether you are or can ever be a good partner. And, if that isn't hurtful and disorienting enough, you start to wonder whether you are even lovable or deserving of love.

At the same time, you start to question your part in the infidelity and ask yourself questions like "Did I drive him to it? Did I not pay enough attention to what was important to him? Did I take him for granted? Was I too hard on him and not understanding enough? Did I neglect him by placing too much attention on the kids or on my job or on myself? Did I not give him enough sex, or sex that was exciting enough?"

Then you experience vacillation as you move to intense feelings of anger and resentment: "How could he do this to me, especially with all that I have done for him and the family? He's so selfish and I have been so naïve. I trusted him. I thought I could trust him. How could I have trusted him?"

And then that goes straight to self-rebuke: "I should have seen this coming; I should have been more attentive. I could have, I should have prevented this." Lastly, self-doubt arrives as you think: "Maybe I expected too much, maybe I don't deserve to be loved. And, worse, maybe I got what I have always feared I deserve."

All of this results in you losing your moorings. You're not sure who you are anymore. Any sense of well-being you had is gone, as is your confidence in your ability to love and be loved. Not only have you totally lost your trust in your partner, but you've also lost much of your trust in yourself. After all, when you began to learn about your partner's betrayal, he likely lied to you and essentially told you not to trust your instincts. If you didn't question him further or if you bought into his cover-up, you now blame your lack of courage to push harder for the truth, which, after all, you didn't want to see or face.

The pain of it all is almost too much: the heartrending hurt, the terrible disappointment, the intense fear, and the towering rage. And it feels like nothing you do can make the pain go away. Nothing.

Well, that's why we wrote this book. While we cannot change what has happened, we can help you get through this terrible time and learn to cope with the pain and the anger. We will help you determine if it's worth giving this relationship a second chance. Most importantly, though we can't take away your current agony, we will teach you how to make sure you never feel it again.

We wrote this book for those who have the strength, the courage, and the love to try to make their relationships work in spite of a partner's infidelity. Over the past twenty-plus years, we've helped numerous couples overcome infidelity, face the trauma, heal from it, and strengthen their love relationships so that they became healthier and happier than they ever were before.

It is possible. It is possible for you.

But it is only possible for you if the conditions are right. The last thing you should do is stay with your partner if there is little or no chance that you can be happy with him again. You do not want to stay with him if he is immature and incapable of loving and committing to you in the way you deserve. There is no way you should be with him if he lacks the courage to be honest with himself as well as with you, and the courage to work through his own weaknesses and unresolved issues. And, lastly, you shouldn't stay with your partner if your relationship has been built on his *need* for you rather than his *love* for you.

TWO TYPES OF LOVE: NEED LOVE VS. BEING LOVE

This is an important distinction for you to be able to make, a key factor in determining whether you should put your time, energy, and precious heart into trying to save your relationship. Psychologist Abraham Maslow (1968) determined that there were two distinct types of love, what he called "need love" and "being love." Maslow defined Need Love as love based on the needs, mainly psychological, that you fulfill for me. That is, Maslow contended that in Need Love, I love you because you take care of my needs, such as my need for love, affection, and sex; my need for security; my need for self-esteem; my need for companionship; and so on.

When my love for you is Being Love, I love you for the person that you are. I see your strengths and your weaknesses and just love the unique package of characteristics that make you up, and I love being with you.

Think of the types of love as two endpoints on a spectrum. Few, if any, relationships are purely Need Love or Being Love; most lie somewhere in between. Those relationships that are closer to the Being Love end of the spectrum are healthier and more likely to last. Those relationships toward the Need Love end of the spectrum are not as healthy, are more volatile, and are less likely to be fulfilling and last.

The reasons for this are relatively clear. If my love for you is based on the needs you fulfill for me, if I find another woman who I think will take care of those needs better than you do, I might very well leave you for her. For example, let's say my self-esteem isn't too great. Well, nothing makes me feel better about myself than when I walk into a party with you on my arm because you're so sexy that all the guys' heads turn to look.

But what if tomorrow I meet a woman whom I find myself really physically attracted to? Maybe being with her would make me feel even better about myself. And what if she's interested in me? My self-esteem neediness coupled with her interest in me may lead me to consider having a fling with her, or leaving you for her and breaking a commitment I made to you.

This is an overly simplistic example, and most people, especially men, are not even aware of how such neediness controls them, but it illustrates the point. Love relationships that are predominantly based on need fulfillment are not built to last. One or most often both partners are psychologically immature and not really ready for a healthy Long-Term Love Relationship (LTLR).

This is not to say that you and your partner cannot have any immaturities or personal weaknesses. We all have such weaknesses and unresolved issues. What we're talking about here is someone who hasn't developed the ability to fulfill his or her own psychological needs. That doesn't mean we should strive toward not needing anyone; we are all social beings and need others. None of us is completely able to fulfill our own psychological needs, just as no relationship, no matter how healthy, is devoid of needs and need fulfillment.

But if we have not traveled very far along the path of developing our respect and love for our self, we are primed for entering into relationships that reflect that poor development or immaturity. These are relationships based more on need than on love. These are relationships at high risk for infidelity and failure.

Evaluating Your Relationship

So how about your relationship? What is your love for each other based on? Is it skewed toward Being Love or Need Love? Where would you put your love for your partner on that spectrum? And where would you put your partner's love for you?

If it is becoming clear to you now that your LTLR is largely based on Need Love, then the possibility of the two of you making each other happy and fulfilled for the long run isn't good.

And just as important, if you see that your love for your partner is based more on Need Love than on Being Love, you need to face the fact that you've got some work to do on yourself. You won't be ready to find the right guy and build a healthy LTLR until you deal with some of your own issues.

WILL HE REALLY OWN UP?

Deciding whether your partner is worth giving another chance will be determined by the answers to two simple questions:

Is he willing to really own his mistakes and weaknesses?

Do you believe he will sincerely work on himself and on his part in the problems in your relationship?

Note that we are not asking if you believe that your partner is going to be setback-free as he accepts this weighty personal and relationship challenge. We are asking if you have faith that he will do his best to work on himself and endure through the rough times that are ahead.

If you answer yes to both these questions, then you believe he is committed to making personal changes and doing his part to heal and fix your LTLR. This is a first indication that you and he have a good chance of rebuilding your relationship so that it is safe from infidelity in the future.

On the other hand, there's a good chance that he's still lying to you about the infidelity. What do you do? Well, continued deceit is an excellent indicator that he really isn't committed to doing what it takes to heal and rebuild your relationship. Unless the lies stop, you should get out. He's not worth it.

WILL YOU OWN UP?

Of course, the flip side of your partner working on himself is that you have to meet him halfway. You have to own and work on your weaknesses and examine how you contributed to the problems in the relationship that helped create the fertile ground for infidelity. Wait. Wait. We're not saying that you're responsible for your partner's infidelity. Not at all. That was your partner's choice. But infidelities don't come from out of nowhere. Invariably there are factors in a relationship that lead to one partner betraying the other. And both partners have a role in those factors. You have to be willing to examine your part and be willing to work on being a better partner, the best partner you can be.

THREE KEY ATTRIBUTES

You're trying to decide whether it's really a good idea for you to try to work it out with your partner, at least for the time being. What are the signs that you and he are really meant for each other and could be blissfully happy together if you could just get past this terrible, awful thing he's done? What are the conditions that need to exist if the two of you are ever going to have a chance to be happy together? It comes down to three attributes. In order for you and your partner to be able to rebuild after this excruciating trauma, the relationship needs love, strength, and courage.

Love

Obviously, each of you still loving the other is vital. At a time like this, one or both of you may not be in touch with your love for the other, to put it mildly. The rage you feel may be blotting out the love you have for him. He may think he loves the other woman and not you anymore.

So one of you may think that you don't love the other any longer. But that doesn't mean that you don't. If you're reading this book, it probably means that you do still love him. The only other possibility is that you feel Need Love for him, and therefore are just desperate not to lose him. If that's the case, it is more important that you work on yourself than on the relationship.

It's also likely that if you're reading this book, you have had some indication from your partner that he wants to reconcile too. If that's the case, there is a good chance that his love for you is still alive. But suffice it to say that unless the love is still there, albeit wounded, there is no good reason to try to save the relationship.

Keep in mind that it takes a lot to kill love. An infidelity, by itself, can't do it. That's right—love is such a powerful force that it usually takes years, most often more than seven to ten, of hurt, pain, disappointment, and anger to kill the love that you once had for your partner.

Strength

Both of you are going to need strength for the road ahead, not only to work through the trauma of his infidelity but also to work on overcoming your individual and relationship weaknesses. It will be very difficult at times for both of you to hang in there and deal with what you have to do in order to put the infidelity behind you.

As the person who has been betrayed, you will need the strength to face your pain, to feel it and talk about it. You will have to resist the urge to curl up in a little ball and escape. And you will need to be strong enough not to use your anger as a bludgeon to hurt your partner for having devastated you so. In turn, your partner must have the strength to weather the storm of your rage and your agony and your terror. He will have to be strong enough to realize that simply saying sorry to you won't make it all better, won't make it all go away.

You will also need the strength not to let your fear control you. Your fear will make you want to run, just leave him, be done with him, and go on to the next guy. It happens all the time. Sometimes it's even the right thing to do. But many times it's not. And at least part of you believes it's not right for you or you wouldn't be reading this book. If you leave him, only do so for the right reasons. And fear is not one of them.

Courage

Courage you are going to need in spades because you are feeling fear in spades. When you let it control you, fear will cause you to have an empty life. One day you'll look back with massive regret because you didn't fully take advantage of the great gift that being alive is. We all want to be safe; we all need to be safe. But safety at the cost of truly living is not worth it. It leads to a gray, colorless, bloodless existence, devoid of passion. You need courage to fight and defeat this fear.

But when we are betrayed, there is an extremely powerful pull to do anything to make ourselves safe again. That's why many of us just run. Run in terror and rage from the person who so wounded us. Don't do it. Don't let your fear control you. Don't leave your partner unless you are convinced that the conditions that would allow the two of you to get over this trauma and be happy together in the future do not exist.

To make the relationship work, one of the most difficult things that you will have to do is trust your partner again. That's right, trust him. Completely. Otherwise, why stay with him? Why be with any man if you're not going to trust him? Having the security of knowing you don't have to worry about being betrayed is a huge part of finding long-term love happiness with anyone.

Finding this trust inside yourself will again require courage. Once he has betrayed you, you'll hardly be inclined to trust him not to do it again. And why should you? He's just shown, in the most terrible way possible, that you can't trust him! You're terrified of trusting him again and rightly so. You don't have to trust him now. You shouldn't trust him now! But at some point you must have the courage to risk giving him your heart wholly and completely and trust him to not break it again.

OUR GUARANTEE

Now, we can't guarantee that the two of you will overcome his horrible betrayal of you and then live happily ever after. That depends on your level of commitment and on his. You may have what it takes, but as you just so agonizingly found out, you can't control your partner. Who knows if he'll hang in there and really work on the relationship, let alone himself.

But, in a way, we can guarantee you a successful journey. That's because no matter what happens with you and your partner, if you work through this book and overcome the pain of the infidelity, we promise that you will grow dramatically as a person. Whether this process leads to your relationship becoming happier and healthier than it ever has been or to an acknowledgment that the relationship has failed, you will become more mature and more psychologically healthy. You'll also be much more likely to have a healthy, fulfilling, and intimate LTLR, whether with your present partner or another. That is a promise.

This book will lead you on that journey, guiding you along this sometimes treacherous but ultimately very fulfilling and meaningful path.

ABOUT THIS BOOK

But before we get started on this journey, let us tell you something about the path you're about to embark upon. This book will help you determine why your partner betrayed you, and will unlock the mystery of how to build, with him, the LTLR that you both yearn for.

One way to think about the approach of this book is to visualize a satellite photo of a continent. We're going to start out with this wide-angle view and will eventually zoom in to your house. The continent represents LTLRs in general. In the first part of the book, we provide you with the secrets to what makes LTLRs work well and what makes them fail. Then we tighten our field of vision to focus on infidelity and what causes it. Then we tighten the field of vision even further to just your house, or in other words, your relationship and your partner's betrayal. Once you have learned the secrets of LTLRs and solved the mystery of why, in particular, your partner betrayed you, we devote the rest of the book to teaching you and your partner how to build a true LTLR.

Infidelities vs. Affairs

You may have already noticed that we talk about "infidelities," not "affairs." Affairs are a type of infidelity. An affair usually lasts over a period of time and includes not just sex but also romantic feelings. Infidelities encompass other types of liaisons, like one-night stands. Whatever the type of infidelity, they're all excruciating. They're all breaches of your trust and of the committed nature of your relationship. The book covers infidelities in general, whether your partner betrayed you through a one-night stand or a long-standing affair.

And it doesn't matter whether you've just found out about your partner's infidelity or if you've known now for a while. You will find this book just as valuable either way. Not only that, you'll find this book useful if your partner had just the one infidelity or multiple ones. If you never want it to happen again, this book is for you.

Who This Book Is Written For

As you've certainly noticed, this book is primarily addressed to a woman whose partner has betrayed her. There are no doubt a number of men who will read this book because their partner has betrayed them. Maybe that's you. If that's the case, we apologize. Just switch the genders used throughout. Chances are, though, that more women will be reading this book than men since more men have infidelities than women, and also because women are more likely to try to save a relationship after an infidelity (Brown 2001, Glass 2003). Women also are more likely to read a self-help book than men are. But we do intend this book to be for men and women alike. You will find the concepts and tools applicable whether you are male or female.

This book is also for married and unmarried couples, and straight, gay, and lesbian couples. Whatever your marital status, the book is about Long-Term Love Relationships in general and is equally applicable to all types of couples. While the examples given all use heterosexual couples, the relationship concepts are just as true for gay and lesbian couples. We hope that any set of partners will be able to learn and grow from reading this book, even if you're in a relatively new love relationship and you want to build it into an LTLR.

To help illustrate the concepts discussed in the book, composites of real couples whom we've worked with over the years are used. To protect their identities, we have changed identifying facts and other details.

Finally, as mentioned earlier, this book is for those whose love partner has been unfaithful and are now committed to trying to make the relationship work. If you have decided that the conditions necessary for overcoming the infidelity do not exist in your relationship, this book can still be vital to your future relationship success. Take the concepts and tools provided here and make sure that you never again feel the agony of betrayal with the man of your dreams.

So here you are. You're reading this book because your partner has been unfaithful to you.

"Fool me once, shame on you."

Okay, you were fooled. But that's it. Not ever again.

The relationship expertise, the self-growth, and all of the tools that you will get from this book will empower you and your relationship so that you will never have to worry about going through this agony again.

"Fool me twice, shame on me."

Won't it be nice never to have to worry about that?

Chapter Review

Two Types of Love

- *Need Love:* based on the needs that you fulfill for me

- *Being Love:* I love you for the person that you are

In order to determine if your relationship is worth saving and working on, you will want to answer the following questions.

Do you each meet the necessary conditions for a second chance?

1. Love: Being Love rather than Need love
   Which type of love do you have?
   - If your love for your partner is based more on Need Love, then you would benefit most from using the tools in the book for yourself before including your partner in the effort. We have found that if you work on being more Being

Love–based, then you are better able to realistically look at yourself and your needs. Then you will be in a stronger position to evaluate your partner's commitment to the effort.

- If you believe your love for your partner is more Being Love, then you are likely to be motivated to try to repair and rebuild the relationship.

- If you believe your partner's love for you is more Need Love, then we recommend that you work on yourself individually and encourage him to do the same. Only when he can more clearly see you for who you are can he decide if he really loves you. If he does not gain this clarity then you risk suffering the first Deal Breaker: one or both people never really loved the other.

2. Do you and your partner have strength: the willingness to weather the ups and downs of both your feelings?

   - If you answer that you have difficulty calming yourself and talking about your feelings rather than blaming and criticizing your partner, then you will benefit from working on the Emotional Self-Awareness Exercise introduced in chapter 5.

3. What about having the courage to really hear the realities of your partner's feelings, experience the full range of your own feelings, and hold both experiences as true? Are you each also willing to face the changes you need to make?

   - If you answer that you have difficulty listening to his feelings, then you will benefit greatly from the Self-Intimacy skills in chapter 5 and the Conflict Intimacy skills presented in chapter 6.

To determine whether your partner is demonstrating earnest motivation, ask yourself the following questions:

- Is he willing to acknowledge and work on his mistakes and weaknesses?

- Is he willing to own his mistakes and make continued best efforts?

- Has he demonstrated either of these qualities in the past?

If you answer no to any of these questions, and particularly the third question, you have reason to be guarded about the likelihood that your partner can change. Nevertheless, if he agrees to work on himself and shows sustained effort over more than three months, there is a good chance that he is earnestly motivated.

chapter 1

now what do I do?

Courage is not the absence of fear, but rather the judgment that something else is more important than fear. —Ambrose Redmoon

So how did you find out?

Was it his e-mail? His cell phone? Text messages? Phone records? Credit card statements? Something more old-fashioned, like lipstick on his collar? Or, maybe the worst: coming home unexpectedly and finding them in your bed? Or did he just come out and tell you?

No matter how you found out, it's devastating. You just learned that you're not the one and only of your one and only. Besides life and death situations, there are few if any more painful experiences than what you're going through right now. Your heart is broken. That description is very appropriate, for not only has your love been betrayed, not only are you in emotional agony, but the pain is so deep that it can literally put you in physical pain and distress.

Your life has been turned upside down. You feel cut adrift, not knowing if you're going to be able to keep your head above water. The familiar, secure foundation that's been the base of your life, that you would give almost anything to have back right now, is gone.

You don't know who he is anymore. He was the one person in your life whom you entrusted your heart to. And now he's taken that precious heart and stomped it underfoot. He was the one person in your life whom you gave your body to. And now he's taken who you are, body and soul, and expressed through his infidelity that you're not enough for him.

You thought that he loved you. Now you don't know. In fact, now you're not even sure if he ever loved you. "How could he do this if he loved me?" His huge deceit casts doubt on everything. You start questioning your experience of him from the moment you met him. Was it all a lie? "Have I been fooling myself all along? How could I be so wrong? How could I have been so oblivious?"

And then you start questioning yourself; you feel disoriented, like you don't know who you are anymore. You're not who you thought you were. Your life isn't what you thought it was. But then, who are you? And where, oh where, is your life going?

Let's start answering those questions. But before you can look forward clearly and chart a healthy course for yourself and your life, you need to look back. You need to understand how you arrived at this awful place.

INFIDELITY 101

So why did this happen to you? Why did your partner do this?

Well, every Long-Term Love Relationship (LTLR) is different. And every person in an LTLR is unique. So generalizations about infidelities, LTLRs, and the individuals involved can be oversimplifications; they can be true for many people but not for you and your partner. Neither are all infidelities the same.

Infidelity Defined

What exactly do we mean when we speak of an "infidelity"? The word's literal meaning refers to the breaking of trust (Lusterman 1998). As we use the term in this book, an infidelity refers to any action taken by a partner in a committed love relationship that violates the agreement of sexual and/or emotional exclusivity.

This general definition applies equally to marital, nonmarital, heterosexual, and homosexual LTLRs. It also clearly states that not all infidelities involve sex. Some infidelities never reach a sexual level, but still can be just as devastating in their emotional betrayal. A partner can become more emotionally intimate with the other woman than he is with his wife. Or he can fall in love with the other woman with or without sex being involved. Some women are more devastated by their betraying partner's emotional involvement with another person than by his sexual involvement. Some find it easier to get past sexual unfaithfulness than emotional unfaithfulness. All of this is said to underscore that any effective definition of infidelity must address the violation of emotional exclusivity just as much as sexual.

The Facts

In our clinical practice of assisting couples to overcome infidelity, we always start by trying to get a grasp on why the infidelity happened and why it happened when it did. The information we gather is placed against the backdrop of the general facts about infidelity that scientific research has generated, especially over the last twenty years, as well as the anecdotal evidence that we have acquired in our years working in this field. So let's begin by sharing those facts with you and then we'll move toward how our concepts about relationships and infidelity apply to you and your LTLR in particular.

Over the past several decades, a number of studies of marital infidelity have compiled and estimated incidence rates. All of them agree on one thing: the incidence of infidelity is quite high.

The numbers range from nearly 50 percent of all marriages (Glass 2003) to 80 percent (Vaughan 1998). And these are just the infidelities that people admit to! It is likely that a number of betraying partners are not honest in their responses to these studies (Spring 1996). Many infidelities may go unreported or denied.

But whatever the exact rate of infidelity in LTLRs, these studies reveal that you are very far from being alone in the trauma that you are currently experiencing. In our "modern" world, more than 50 percent of all LTLRs are impacted, interrupted, and shattered by one form of infidelity or another. It is therefore more likely that either you or your partner will break the agreement of emotional or sexual fidelity than it is that neither of you will ever do so.

Not only that, but since most of us have been in at least a few love relationships, almost all of us have either been unfaithful or had our partner be unfaithful to us at least once. So you are very definitely not alone. And we authors are no exception. We've been there. We've suffered that. So both personally and professionally, we know a bit about what you're going through and we're committed to helping you through it.

HOW DO YOU MAKE DECISIONS TODAY?

It has been said that time is a great healer. This will be especially true right now in your life. While you vacillate between rage, loss, revenge, and desperation to have him back, time will help you feel less crazy and see what is real. With the passage of time and the abatement of the immediate intense reactions, you will know better what you feel about him, learn from him how he feels about you, and be able to assess the contribution you each made to the relationship's stresses and strains.

Keep in mind that it's often counterproductive to make a life-changing decision when you are in the throes of anger. We advise that you do not decide to divorce or end the relationship right away, when you are so full of hurt and rage. On the other hand, deciding to separate temporarily can make good sense. You or your partner could move in with a family member or friend for a short while. Put off making permanent new housing arrangements to next week or next month.

Quick action is often retaliatory or an attempt at control. However, impulsive actions are often just that, and do not bring you any genuine power over the situation. Being quiet and sitting in the immediate reality of the loss and hurt can be the most genuine way to experience a kind of control. This allows you to begin to answer that pivotal question: should I give him a second chance?

During this time of utter confusion, take comfort and strength in the normalcy of your routines such as exercise classes, lunching with friends, and regular manicure appointments and other self-pampering activities. You will probably feel like you are in a fog, but maintaining your habits will eventually bring you a sense of safety and the realization that life continues.

If you have children, it's also essential that you keep up their normal routines. They need to feel stable even as they see or feel that something catastrophic has happened; they can't help but be aware that you are bereft and shaken. For their sake, you need to cry and talk and yell away from your children. The conflict is between you and your partner, not them. You don't want your children to feel like they're in the middle.

We know how hard it is to contain your feelings, and we also know how frightening it is for children to see their mother or father so afraid and angry. The more you can maintain some of the family's normalcy, and the sooner you can regain some of your emotional footing, the more your children will be insulated from the chaos and pain.

To help yourself make sense of this difficult time, share your feelings and thoughts with friends who can offer you wisdom, compassion, and support. Choose a close friend who is able to comfort you, hug you, listen while you rail, and ask you questions to help you think as well as feel.

Your Desire for Revenge

We recommend that you do not immediately confide in your parents, your partner's family, or his friends. While this may be very tempting, such disclosure at this point would be mostly retaliatory. Safeguard your integrity by not using what you say to others as a way to get back at him. This does not mean that we advocate keeping the betrayal a secret from those you are close to, just that you make sure anger and the desire to retaliate are not your primary motivations for including these people in your confidence.

And by all means, think long and hard, and get the counsel of people you really respect and trust, before you consider telling your children about his infidelity. During this time when your emotions are running so high, it's simply not a good idea to tell your children—no matter their age. After all, your husband is their parent (or stepparent) and your marital disruption represents a loss and a threat to them. You'd probably be telling them to get back at your partner, and using your children that way is never okay. It makes them into innocent victims.

Remember, your desire for revenge is not unusual. When we are hurt, we often respond with angry feelings as a way to feel less vulnerable. It is important, however, to realize that having an urge for revenge is vastly different from taking action. Acting on these thoughts and desires is not right or healthy for you. To process these feelings, you could try writing about them in a journal.

However, if you find that writing about your pain makes you more enraged, more desirous of revenge, then obviously this exercise is not helpful for you. You might be better served by making a list of the healthy options you have for dealing with pain. What tactics have you used in the past to work through and diminish hurt and anger? Use these strategies rather than lashing out in hopes of revenge.

Sending angry e-mails or poison pen letters to your partner, contacting the other woman or her spouse out of anger, telling your children in order to damage their relationship with their father, and other such revenge-motivated actions ultimately hurt you and make immediate matters worse. We know that avoiding these temptations is easier said than done. We respect that reality. But we're here to remind you that what you feel is justified and that you are not crazy or deserving of being betrayed. We know that in time you will regain your equilibrium, which will help you recognize that you will find your way again. You will be able to make some sense of this hurt. Reacting purely out of anger only begets more anger and hurt. And right now you need to comfort yourself rather than depleting your limited emotional resources on actions that do not ultimately benefit you.

SHOULD YOU EVER TRUST HIM AGAIN?

Working through your anger isn't the only challenge you face. Getting past your partner's infidelity doesn't just mean that he ends it with the other woman. It doesn't just mean that he promises never to do it again. A key aspect of getting the infidelity behind is you dealing with your fear of trusting your partner again. There are few more effective ways to torpedo the possibility of saving your LTLR than to let this very natural and healthy fear control you. Becoming a suspicious, controlling partner in order to protect yourself from being betrayed again will backfire. Instead of making you safer, this kind of fear-motivated behavior will create fertile ground for more betrayal.

You have every right to demand that going forward your partner is accountable for being open with you about his activities. This full disclosure is one of the things that will provide you with day-to-day reassurance that your partner is trustworthy again. And you have the right to ask him not to do things that would heighten your fear of further betrayal (see chapter 12). But taking this too far, trying to cage him so that there is no danger of repeat betrayal, will lead to ruin.

So while your fear is healthy, letting it control you over the long term is not. This is one of the most central, important, difficult, and scary choices that anyone who has been betrayed by their partner's infidelity is faced with: do I ever trust him again?

Clearly, it is not wise to trust your partner again right away. Part of you may want to. Part of you wants to believe that this was just an aberration, that he really does love you and would never hurt you like this again. Even if this is true, it doesn't mean you should turn around and put your faith and trust in your partner any time soon. Trust has to be earned over time. Your partner must show through his words and with his actions that he does love you, that he is committed to you, that he means what he says, and that he does what he says he is going to do.

But if your partner does talk the talk and walk the walk, and does so for a while, then you've got a big choice to make. Do you let go of your fear and take the risk of trusting him again? If your partner has really taken responsibility for his betrayal and relationship weaknesses and worked sincerely on overcoming them, and if he has sincerely engaged in trust-building behaviors, he's made *your* choice of trusting him again easier, less scary.

TRUSTING YOURSELF AGAIN

So much of your choice to trust your partner again depends on him. But a lot of it depends on you, on your ability to summon the courage to confront your fear and not let it control you. Not only that, you have to be able to trust yourself. You were fooled, hoodwinked. You trusted him and he abused that trust and betrayed you in the most painful way possible. How can you trust yourself not to be duped again?

We can help you there.

Self-Intimacy

There are two powerful ways for you to build back your trust in yourself and the first has nothing to do with your partner—it depends totally on you. You need to start by really knowing yourself, in particular, being emotionally self-aware. This means having a conscious understanding of your feelings and what they mean, and trusting your instincts.

In chapter 5, we will teach you about the importance of this emotional self-awareness, what we call "Self-Intimacy." This is the key for any of us to be able to take good care of ourselves and stand up for ourselves when needed. We will share with you a powerful tool that you can use to develop your Self-Intimacy. By becoming self-intimate, you will become keenly aware of your emotions and what they mean for you and for your LTLR. You will learn to listen to your instincts. And so you will grow strong in your trust in yourself, and that trust will be very well placed. Consequently, you will become very, very difficult to hoodwink again.

Conflict Intimacy

Regaining trust in yourself and your relationship also depends on you attaining the ability to know when your LTLR is starting to get into trouble. If the problems aren't dealt with they'll grow, and then your relationship can again become vulnerable to infidelity. You need to learn how to recognize when you and your partner aren't dealing with your differences and conflicts well. That's the red flag for you to look for, the sign that if you don't do something you could be entering the infidelity danger zone.

We have found that infidelities are pretty predictable if you know how to read these signs. This doesn't mean that all infidelities are preventable, nor does it mean that the infidelity was your fault because you didn't see the signs. We each have enough trouble exerting control over ourselves; our control of another person, even our life partner, is marginal at best. So there's no ironclad way of guaranteeing that your partner will never stray again. But we're going to teach you how to get very good at preventing it from ever happening again.

This begins with learning to recognize when factors creating a vulnerability to infidelity are emerging in your LTLR. Without exception, these factors are always related to a breakdown of emotional intimacy between you and your partner. There will be a perceptible change in the level of openness and honesty and your ability to share your feelings, positive and negative, about things going on in your lives that are both related and unrelated to your relationship.

The acid test of emotional intimacy in an LTLR is how well a couple deals with conflict. The more trouble a couple has in dealing with conflict and the differences that naturally exist between them, the more they're creating fertile soil from which an infidelity can sprout. Because your partner has already been unfaithful, the two of you must not have dealt with tension well in your LTLR. What's more, we're sure that your relationship fits into one of two maladaptive conflict styles.

Two gifted couples therapists call these styles Hostile Dependent and Conflict Avoidant (Bader and Pearson 1988). The Hostile Dependent couple gets locked into cycles of toxic conflict, dealing with their differences by having destructive arguments that resolve nothing and add insult to injury by further hurting each other with shouted words. Conflict Avoidant couples do anything they can so as not to fight, brushing everything under the rug and hoping it goes away. Of course, it never does. Which style fits the two of you?

Whether you developed a Hostile Dependent or a Conflict Avoidant style, when you and your partner started not dealing with conflict well, you began planting the seeds of infidelity vulnerability. Negative emotions built up and festered between you. Disappointment and resentment grew. Instead of growing closer and more intimate, over time you started drifting, separating, alienating. The signs of discontent were there, but you didn't see them, or you minimized their meaning. And then the unthinkable happened: out of an unnoticed failed conflict process came unseen infidelity.

In chapter 6, we'll teach you how to become conflict intimate, how to deal with differences in a healthy way so that conflict actually serves to make your LTLR stronger, not weaker. In so doing, your Conflict Intimacy will make your LTLR infidelity invulnerable. You and your partner will get good at strengthening the intimacy that exists between you, building a powerful wall of defense against the temptation of an infidelity.

Much of this book is about building a healthy Long-Term Love Relationship with your partner, because in the final analysis, a strong, fulfilling LTLR is the surest way to prevent infidelity. Chapters 3 through 7 are devoted to explaining the simple cornerstones of healthy LTLRs and teaching you how to use those concepts to build your dream LTLR with your partner. The ideas we share with you are not complex, nor are they out of your reach. They consist of tools—some relating to your relationship with yourself, some relating to your relationship with your partner— that are eminently learnable. You don't need to be a rocket scientist or a psychologist to understand or become proficient at them. That may be the best thing about this relationship stuff: almost all of us are capable of getting good at it, of becoming a great love partner, of building a loving and fulfilling LTLR.

We'll show you how your emotional self-awareness will keep you tuned into cracks developing in your relationship's intimacy. We'll teach you how to recognize when signs of infidelity vulnerability are appearing in your LTLR, and we'll school you in how to deal with them effectively. With Self Intimacy and Conflict Intimacy, instead of blithely and blindly traveling down the slippery slope into betrayal, you will be building a stronger, more resilient, and cherished relationship that safeguards itself.

THE THREE TYPES OF INFIDELITIES

But that's not where you are right now. You're in relationship hell. So once we teach you how to build a rock-solid foundation for your LTLR, the rest of the book deals specifically with the causes of infidelity, the different types of infidelity, and then most importantly, the prevention of infidelity.

In our work with couples we've found that there are three types of infidelity. These types are not defined by sexual content or length of time, but rather by what caused the infidelity. We categorize infidelities by the major emotion in the betraying person that motivates him or her to be unfaithful.

We find this approach powerful because it not only affords a simple description explaining the infidelity, but it also indicates what the underlying cause of the infidelity was within the betraying partner and within the LTLR. It pinpoints the weaknesses in both. Thinking about infidelities this way will help you to focus your energy in healing your LTLR.

In chapters 8 through 11, we detail the three types of infidelity: Infidelity of Fear, Infidelity of Loneliness, and Infidelity of Anger. We'll talk about how to recognize the precursors leading to each type of infidelity. We'll describe the causes of each type and then we'll discuss what you can do to make your LTLR safe from a reoccurrence of those circumstances.

DO I STAY OR DO I GO?

You're reading this book because you're in pain, you want to do whatever you can to never feel this pain again, *and* you love your partner and don't want to give up on him. We applaud you. The easy thing to do is give up and run away. Sometimes that's even the right thing. But we've found that very often the easy thing isn't also the right thing. This is especially true in LTLRs. So many people get divorced when it isn't necessary: if they had only had the courage to own their weaknesses and mistakes and sincerely work on changing, they could have saved their LTLR and been the happier for it. But to many of us it's too scary to take an honest look at ourselves, to confront our own demons. So we run.

All too often "irreconcilable differences" really means "I don't have the courage to face my weaknesses and to acknowledge my contributions to the problems."

The Three Deal Breakers

In fact, in all our years of working with couples, we've only found three things that absolutely doom an LTLR. We call them the Three Deal Breakers:

1. One or both partners were never in love with the other.

2. Over a long period of time, usually more than seven years, so much anger and hurt were inflicted by one or both partners on the other that it killed the love that once was there.

③ One or both partners refuse to own their part in the difficulties in the LTLR and/or they refuse to sincerely work on themselves and their contributions to the relationship's problems.

These three deal breakers are the only things that LTLRs cannot overcome. Unless they fall into the second category, infidelity is not on the list, drug and alcohol abuse are not on the list, and physical abuse is not on the list. Money trouble isn't. A sexual problem is not. Parenting stress is not.

If caught in time, all of those problems can be overcome if the third deal breaker does not apply. That is, if both partners are willing to own their part in those problems and sincerely work on themselves to overcome them, all troubles can be conquered if they aren't allowed to fester for too many years.

If you look long and hard at your LTLR and you are sure that one of these deal breakers applies, then the best thing for you to do is to end the relationship with as much dignity and respect as possible, mourn the loss of it, and then move on with your life.

But if after sober examination of your LTLR, you don't think any of the deal breakers applies, or you're not sure, then work as hard as you can to make it work. Even if you try your best to heal your LTLR and you end up terminating the relationship because one of the deal breakers does exist, you will leave with a clean conscience knowing you gave it your all. We've worked with many people, and you may know some yourself, who regret leaving their LTLRs without giving them a chance.

Don't do that unless you know one of the deal breakers applies. Infidelity can be overcome.

Don't Give Up Too Soon

What we advise our clients, and what we're advising you, is that unless you are sure one of the deal breakers applies to your LTLR, don't give up. Many couples come to us after an infidelity has been revealed and one or both of the partners thinks the second deal breaker is true for them. They don't think they love their partner anymore. You may be feeling this way now, in the midst of all your pain and anger. But when many of these couples work on repairing the damage done in the LTLR, when both of them do their part in this effort, they find that their love comes blossoming back to life. So consider this carefully before you decide for sure that you don't love your partner anymore. Your love for him ay just be masked by all the hurt and rage you feel right now.

We have great respect and admiration for anyone who makes e difficult choice to work on their LTLR. This is a choice to honor the commitment you made to your partner, to yourself, and to your relationship. Too often nowadays people look to take the easy way out. But not you. You're choosing to try your best in the face of great pain, even though you don't know if you will achieve your goal of rebuilding and achieving a loving, fulfilling LTLR with your partner.

THE WORK AHEAD OF YOU

One thing that you're going to have to face squarely in this healing process is that it's not only about your partner changing. If you are really sincere in your commitment to make your LTLR work, you must take a cold hard look at yourself as well. You're going to have to take responsibility for your faults and for your mistakes in the relationship. You're going to have to work as hard as you can to become a better love partner. And as we spoke about earlier in this chapter, you're going to have to work on taking better care of yourself, on improving your relationship with yourself, on strengthening your Self-Intimacy. If, and only if, you really work on these two relationships, the one with your partner and the one with yourself, will you have any chance of making your LTLR work.

Of course, your partner's going to have to do the same. Plus he's got to earn your trust back and make amends for his betrayal. He's got to come up big after what he's done. And you're both going to have to work hard not only on yourselves but also on your relationship, your communication, your Conflict Intimacy (chapter 6), and your Affection Intimacy (chapter 7).

We guarantee that if the two of you do these things, and if none of the deal breakers apply, you will be able to build a Long-Term Love Relationship full of love and joy and fulfillment. It will take all your strength and your courage, and your partner's. But you *can* do it. This book will show you the way.

Chapter Review

Can your relationship be characterized by one of these conflict styles?

Maladaptive Conflict Styles

- *Conflict Avoidant:* These couples do anything they can so as not to fight, brushing everything under the rug and hoping it goes away.

Is this your relationship? If so, developing Self-Intimacy (chapter 5) and Conflict Intimacy (chapter 6) will help you break out of this pattern.

- *Hostile Dependent:* These couples get locked into cycles of toxic conflict, dealing with their differences by having destructive arguments. Instead of resolving anything, these couples usually just add insult to injury by further hurting each other with their shouted words.

If this pattern describes your relationship, then you will both benefit from being more self-intimate (chapter 5) and will need to work both individually and together to become conflict intimate (chapter 6). You will find the Maturity Goals Handout (appendix C) to be most helpful to you.

Do any of the Three Deal Breakers apply to your relationship?

1. One or both partners never loved the other.

2. Too many disappointments and too much pain in the relationship.

3. One or both partners are unwilling to acknowledge and take responsibility for his/her negative contribution to the relationship.

   If number 1 appears to apply, be careful. Right now your world is upside down. We recommend that you give yourself at least twelve weeks before making a decision to divorce or end the relationship. A separation and time to work on yourself may be the best course of action. Reviewing the material in chapter 2 and 3 about what to do can really help you separate your traumatic feelings from the earlier positive feelings.
   If number 2 seems applicable, then do not act rashly. This is a very difficult time. We advise you to take a few months to get some perspective on the entirety of the relationship. Chapters 2 and 3 can be especially helpful as you evaluate whether to invest the necessary energy into the relationship. We also recommend that you read the entire book before you make any decision. That way you'll know that any decision to end your relationship won't be mostly influenced by anger or a sense of victimization but can be one made after clear-headed reflection.
   If number 3 seems to apply, you'll know best once you start to work on yourself and ask your partner to work on himself. Be careful not to jump to conclusions; he is likely to be defensive. Give the relationship ninety days of concerted effort to change the way you talk about difficulties and your feelings. During those ninety days, make a commitment to doing the Emotional Self-Awareness Exercise (chapter 5) and the I-to-I exercise (chapter 6) with or without your partner's involvement, and then ask yourself if the third deal breaker applies.

chapter 2

companions on this journey: couples who have been there

There are no "good" or "bad" people. Some are a little better or a little worse, but all are activated more by misunderstanding than malice.
—Tennessee Williams

However you choose to respond to your partner's betrayal, know that you are not alone. Others have made the same choices, done the same things before you. As you know, many, many people have found themselves in the same painful and confusing place where you now find yourself. Fortunately for you, what they went through can help you in your struggle to move forward.

As we guide you through the work of healing yourself and rebuilding your relationship, you will be accompanied by four couples who have been there. We will use their Long-Term Love Relationship stories to demonstrate the paths that can be taken when faced with the relationship challenges that arise when a partner has been unfaithful.

These four couples are composites of the many couples we have helped over the last twenty-plus years. You will likely recognize yourself, your partner, and your relationship in one or more of the couples. While each of us is unique, the challenges we face in relationships and the options we have for responding are much alike.

Our four couples make the concepts for constructing a stronger and infidelity-resistant relationship come to life. They will help you see the paths you have taken, the crossroads you have come to, and the choices that lie ahead of you. In learning their stories, you will better understand how you and your partner arrived here and how to never again return to this place of hurt and betrayal. Let's introduce you to them now.

■ Gracie and Jake: An Infidelity of Fear

Theirs was a good match, opposites attracting. Both Gracie and Jake are in their mid-thirties. Gracie works as a personal assistant to a corporate executive while Jake is the CEO of another corporation. She is outgoing and high energy while he grounds her with his stability and steadfastness. They chose each other because of their mutual attraction and similar goals. They have been married for ten years and have two children, to whom they are both devoted. But recently, Gracie and Jake have found that their interests are becoming more and more different. After ten years some such differences are to be expected.

They've always had spats, but these usually fizzle out before becoming full-blown arguments because Jake withdraws after stating his view and Gracie then just drops the topic. Gracie experiences Jake as doing what he wants no matter what she says. So over the years Gracie has become resentful of Jake's dominance in their "mutual" decisions while Jake has become more and more withdrawn from Gracie as well as covertly resentful of her for "leaving the solutions" to him.

Gracie grew up in an intact family with one older sister. She was very close with her father, yet felt like she had to work hard to earn his attention and interest. She is an attractive woman who appears to have a high degree of self-confidence. Gracie enjoys spending time with friends and family. She is well liked by others for her willingness to pitch in when help is needed. She clearly enjoys being appreciated by others. Jake was attracted to Gracie's confidence and her appreciation of his strengths.

Jake is an oldest son and very responsible. He grew up in a supportive family that didn't talk much about feelings. As a result, Jake is a compassionate and caring partner but he is not very emotionally expressive. He is admired by many for his follow-through and reliability. Gracie was attracted to Jake's ability to take on and solve problems and to his steadfastness. Jake enjoys helping others.

Jake has just learned that Gracie has been having an affair for more than a year. Jake discovered the affair by coming upon some e-mails sent between his wife and another man. Jake never believed that Gracie would betray him. He is just beginning to learn that she has had several infidelities over the past eight years. He's in shock, but not so much that he isn't also very angry.

Gracie began to have affairs as she found herself feeling afraid in the marriage: afraid of boredom, afraid of not being attractive enough, and afraid of being invisible to Jake. These feelings grew after the birth of her children. She felt engulfed by the demands of being a parent and she had a strong need to know that other men found her desirable.

She has been able to keep the affairs hidden because she has told herself that they had nothing to do with her marriage. She has even tried to talk herself into believing that her affairs have helped her be a better partner for Jake in some ways, or at the least that they have enabled her to stay in the marriage. Ironically, Gracie tells Jake that she knows he is a very good man. Now that Jake has discovered the affairs and confronted her, Gracie feels ashamed and doesn't understand why she has treated him and their relationship so horribly.

■ Samantha and Paul: An Infidelity of Loneliness

"Two peas in a pod," people would often say about them. Samantha and Paul met in college and married soon thereafter. They are in their mid-forties and have been together for more than twenty years. Both are good-looking, high-energy people who seemed to be perfect for each other.

However, with Paul's full-time finance career and Samantha's part-time paralegal career, the couple has been struggling to get along, especially since the birth of their third child. For example, they often have difficulty seeing eye to eye on finances. No matter what the point of contention, Samantha and Paul have real trouble ever resolving their differences. Paul states that he tries to talk to Samantha about his unhappiness and frustration and feels she does not value his feelings and complaints. Samantha believes that she has been trying to make the changes Paul wants but often experiences him as being too critical and angry.

When the two of them get into disagreements, Paul starts out easygoing, but then quickly gets very angry in response to any perceived criticism. When Samantha then backs down and gets quiet, Paul is glad that the argument is over but also feels frustrated as he realizes that no resolution has been reached.

Samantha is the youngest child from an intact family. She describes her relationship with her family as good. She always aspired to marry and have children. She holds some grudges against people who have disappointed her, but generally she comes across as optimistic. She will speak up when she does not like something, but if Paul gets too angry, she will clam up and become quietly resentful.

Paul's parents divorced when he was in high school. He is the third of four children. He admits to feeling alone while growing up, but was pretty successful in school and friendships. He has always wanted to have a close family and a wife who was his best friend.

Samantha recently discovered that Paul was having an affair with a woman at work. Some telltale signs led to suspicion, which then led to her examining his cell phone bills. Paul is angry with himself for hurting his wife and for betraying his own values. He contends that he did not look for an affair. After working with Mary for more than a year, he found that he felt more alive in her presence. This eventually convinced him that something significant was missing in his marriage. The vibrancy he experienced with Mary became overwhelming and he became both emotionally and sexually involved with her. Samantha is devastated.

■ Amy and Lewis: An Infidelity of Anger

"Lots of chemistry" is how people would describe Amy and Lewis. They've always had a lot in common and there is a lot of energy between them. Amy is an attorney and Lewis is a stockbroker. Sometimes their chemistry would be positively and passionately charged, but sometimes it would become negative and very tense. They've dealt with conflict by either openly arguing or by trying to avoid "hot" topics. At their worst, they would allow unresolved anger and resentment to smolder between them. Despite this negative pattern, they have been committed to one another for fifteen years. They are both in their fifties.

Amy is a very well-respected woman in her profession. She was married once before when she was younger, and had no children from that marriage. Early on, she and Lewis decided not to have children as well. When she met Lewis, she was attracted to his accomplishments and his high energy.

Amy grew up in a very achievement-oriented family where much was expected of all members. She felt sorry for her mom, who allowed Amy's father to dominate, and had contradictory feelings for her dad as she admired his strength while resenting how he would assert his position in the family. As Amy grew up, she wanted a husband and family and promised herself that she would be a strong woman and marry a strong but kind man.

When she and Lewis get into arguments, she starts out strong and asserts her opinion, but as he "antes up" to her strength, she resorts to mean and hurtful comments or she withdraws with great resentment. She later expresses her continuing anger by giving him the cold shoulder or presenting herself as the wounded party.

Lewis is the eldest son from an unhappy marriage. He has mixed feelings about both of his parents, although he is more likely to say that he has no real strong feelings toward either of them. He comes across as bright and capable, but seems to never be fully present. It's as if he's holding back in the conversation or relationship. He is accomplished and enjoys his many successes. While he does argue with Amy, he will tell you that he dislikes arguments and tension and would prefer that they not occur. He believes he only argues to try to get her to stop.

While Amy and Lewis fight and argue often, they are still invested in their relationship. Both have often been suspicious of the other's faithfulness, but this is only brought up in the heat of arguments. Recently Amy came across some phone and credit card records that didn't make sense. These raised her suspicions and she confronted Lewis. He denied any inappropriate actions and accused Amy of being crazy and overreacting. However, after more pushing and asking and accusing, Lewis admitted to having an infidelity. That was one month ago. Since then Amy has done more investigating and has confronted him with damning e-mails. As a result, Lewis has finally come clean and admitted that over the last twelve years he has been with prostitutes, had some one-night stands, and even had a more prolonged affair.

Lewis admits that his actions are wrong and hurtful, but also states that he feels he had no choice. He asserts that Amy's constant moods and anger led him to find solace in other women. Amy is enraged by his betrayals.

■ Cindy and Scott: Growing Pains Without Infidelity

They are often described as a likable couple who have a lot going for them. Cindy and Scott met in their late twenties through friends; they are now in their forties. Cindy is a school principal while Scott is an English professor. Their backgrounds are very different, but their values are similar. When they married, they felt their differences enriched their life together. Over the years, the dissimilarities in their family histories posed many challenges to them both individually and as a couple. These conflicts emerged in a variety of areas, including how to deal with the expectations of their extended families, how to resolve disagreements, and their differing comfort levels with how much emotions are expressed.

Cindy is the middle of three children and the oldest daughter. Her parents had a good marriage, but when she was ten years old her father died suddenly. She and her siblings and mother were all rocked by this loss. About two years later her mother remarried. Over the next few years, Cindy and her siblings incorporated their stepfather into their family and life became stable and safe again. While Cindy loves her stepfather, she has some fears of loss in her romantic relationships and has been determined to be independent and self-supporting in case she has to take care of herself. She is very driven, high energy, and generally optimistic.

Cindy was attracted to Scott because he reminded her of her deceased father: both are Armenian and professionals in similar fields of work. While the couple is intellectually similar, their family backgrounds are socioeconomically different. Cindy's family has more education and is upper middle class while Scott's is more blue collar and lower middle class. Cindy grew up knowing about family differences and believed that Scott would work with her to make their relationship better.

Scott is the eldest of three children. His family and extended family are close and proud of their Armenian heritage. His parents' marriage was strong, while not always happy. His mother was the dominant parent and could be moody and demanding. Scott was always a successful student and, unlike his siblings, had academic aspirations. While he was motivated to excel, he was also something of an introvert with a biting and sarcastic sense of humor. He was attracted to the similarities between himself and Cindy, and liked how outgoing and bright she was.

Over the eighteen years they have been together, Cindy and Scott have had many challenges both personally and as a couple. Their relationship has been tense, rocked to the core at times by extended family differences, and yet remained resilient. Neither one of them has had an infidelity. While they have alternated between avoiding their problems, yelling about them, and relenting and agreeing to halfhearted solutions in order to end stalemates, they have continued the marriage and came to therapy with the hopes of learning a better way to face their differences and troublesome emotions.

LEARNING FROM THE FOUR COUPLES

Each of these couples will come along with you as you reconstruct your Long-Term Love Relationship. You'll see what they went through. You'll see what mistakes they made and why. In their strengths and weaknesses, you'll see some of yours as well as those of your partner. You'll learn from them how to use your strengths to overcome your weaknesses. Through them, you will see the outcomes of the various choices ahead of you.

As you have noticed, three of the couples are dealing with infidelity while the fourth is not. Despite the challenges and mistakes that all romantic relationships inevitably face, Cindy and Scott will serve to illustrate for you the path leading to a strong and enduring LTLR free of infidelity.

Chapter 2: Companions on this Journey

Gracie & Jake: An Infidelity of Fear

- They are in their thirties and have been married ten years.

- They have two children

- After having children Gracie, began to feel bored, afraid of becoming invisible, and vaguely dissatisfied with herself. She had no awareness of what she'd describe as legitimate complaints about her marriage.

- She began having long-term affairs when her children were young.

- She described the affairs as love affairs and saw them as satisfying needs that she could not expect her husband to meet.

- Jake was completely unaware of Gracie's infidelities.

- This couple looked content and happy on the outside, and both would have reported the same.

Samantha & Paul: An Infidelity of Loneliness

- They are in their forties and have been married for twenty years.

- They have three children.

- They struggle within the marriage with financial issues and priorities.

- Both admit some dissatisfactions in the marriage, but both are committed to the relationship.

- After more than ten years of marriage Paul was surprised and confused by his strong attraction to another woman at work. He was not looking for an affair but eventually became romantically and sexually involved with the woman.

Amy & Lewis: An Infidelity of Anger

- They are in their fifties and have been married for fifteen years.

- They have no children.

- They have a very passionate marriage, which, at its worst, erupts with great anger over many issues that do not get resolved.

- Lewis views his wife as angry and withholding, and he is angry at her for this treatment.

- Very soon in the relationship he engages in a variety of infidelities and justifies them as Amy's fault for the way she treats him.

- He feels justified in his actions.

Cindy & Scott: Growing Pains Without Infidelity

- They are in their forties and have been married for eighteen years.

- They have similar values and educational experiences.

- Their family ethnic backgrounds is part of their mutual attraction

- They struggle with differences arising from their respective families and their methods of communicating. They vacillate between avoiding their problems and getting bogged down in them.

- They have pursued marriage counseling as Cindy has found herself feeling unhappy and resentful in the marriage.

- Neither of them has considered having an affair despite the dissatisfaction and frustrations each feels with the relationship.

chapter 3

the stages of love: why he betrayed you when he did

Heat is required to forge anything. Every great accomplishment is the story of a flaming heart.
—Arnold H. Glasgow

"Why now? After all we've been through together, why did he do this now?" This is one of the biggest questions we ask when our partner has betrayed us. We obsess endlessly on it because in most cases we don't have an answer. We start questioning everything that's happened recently. "Was it something I did? Something I didn't do? What signs did I miss?" And on and on and on, you keep questioning yourself and your relationship.

Well, the good news is that we're going to tell you why it happened when it did. Over the years, working with couple after couple, we've actually discovered that the "when" of an infidelity is very predictable. Predictable because the answer to "why now?" is always the same! Infidelities always happen at the same point in a Long-Term Love Relationship. Always.

But to know what that point is, how to see it coming, and how to recognize when you're there, you first have to understand that all the phases in LTLRs are connected. And you have to understand *how* they're connected.

THE DEVELOPMENTAL MODEL OF LONG-TERM LOVE RELATIONSHIPS

Long-Term Love Relationships grow and develop over time, just like individuals do. And just like individuals, LTLRs go through definable, predictable stages of growth that are marked by beginnings, endings, and recognizable characteristics.

We've found that you can't have insight into what's going on in an LTLR if you don't understand the growth process that all LTLRs go through. Furthermore, without knowing where a couple is in the life span of their LTLR, you're handicapped in understanding what they're doing and why they're doing it.

If you understand the developmental stages of LTLRs, it becomes clear why things are happening, when things should be happening, and what comes next. Through learning about the LTLR developmental process, you will come to realize why your partner's betrayal happened when it did. And this will go a long way in helping you to ensure that it never happens again.

So what is this LTLR growth process? We call it the Developmental Model of Long-Term Love Relationships. A few other couples therapists have pioneered this love relationship development concept. Our model grows out of the work of Ellyn Bader and Peter Pearson (1988, 2000), whose books about couples we recommend to you.

The developmental model we use in working with couples consists of four stages: Sweet Symbiosis, Soured Symbiosis, Differentiation, and Synergy. After we define and describe each of them for you, we'll get back to and answer that burning question, "Why did he do this now?"

Stage 1: Sweet Symbiosis

And, oh, how sweet it is! This is the magical time of falling in love, one of the most wonderful experiences in anyone's life. During this initial honeymoon period of your LTLR, you and your partner were filled with feelings of love and passion for each other. You felt such joy in having found him and in being with him. You couldn't stop thinking about him when you were apart and couldn't wait till you saw him again. During this stage, you experienced the joy of unconditionally giving and being given to. Anything seemed possible and you were filled with happiness to have found in him this "missing part" of yourself. You both were so, so happy.

Stage 1 is symbiotic functioning at its intoxicating best. But what is "symbiosis"? The dictionary defines it as "the living together in more or less intimate association or close union of two dissimilar organisms," or more specifically for our purposes, "a relationship between two people in which each person is dependent upon and receives reinforcement, whether beneficial or detrimental, from the other" (*Random House Dictionary* 1987).

So symbiosis is about dependency. That doesn't sound like a good thing. But dependency and symbiosis get a bad rap; we're all dependent beings to one extent or another. Overdependence isn't good, but dependence is normal and healthy for us humans. Many therapists think of symbiosis as a negative thing, but it's not necessarily so. Just ask anyone who is in stage 1!

In fact, each of us is driven at a very deep, instinctual level to bond with another, to create this dependency and to build this symbiosis. It's rooted in how we evolved in order to guarantee the survival of our species. It's easy to see that species survival, for *Homo sapiens* as well as many other species, is greatly enhanced if two adults not only mate but remain bonded to each other for at least some period of time. This increases the survival chances of their young since two adults working together can provide care, safety, and sustenance at a much higher level than can a sole parent. In humans, our emotions such as love and jealousy have evolved to help cement this bond.

But what does symbiosis have to do with falling in love? Well, when two people are in the Sweet Symbiosis stage, the symbiotic nature of their bond causes them to minimize their differences and overlook what each of them doesn't like in the other. This is the meaning of the famous saying, "Love is blind." You don't truly "see" each other. You're focused on the wonderful parts of who your partner is and are oblivious or nearly so of his faults. This selective vision helps you fall in love. After all, since he's so wonderful, why wouldn't you fall in love with him? He's so perfect that you can't keep yourself from falling in love with him!

Of course, nobody's perfect. So the great joy and happiness of the initial Sweet Symbiosis stage of LTLRs is partly based on the fantasy that you two are ideal for each other. But no couple is so well matched that they are perfect for each other. No couple is so well suited that they don't inevitably hurt, disappoint, and anger each other.

The intrusion of this fact into the reality of your relationship heralds the end of Sweet Symbiosis. When the fantasy component inherent in two people falling in love starts to butt up against the reality of their real weaknesses, mistakes, and differences, stage 1 comes to a close, the rose-colored glasses come off.

Research into the brains of people who are in Sweet Symbiosis is beginning to reveal that there is a flood of pleasure chemicals in our brains at this time, helping to create the blissful fog of falling head over heals in love. But nobody, and no brain, evidently, can sustain this flood of pleasure forever.

But it is very important to note that even though this first, romantic stage of LTLRs is partly based on fantasy, it is a very healthy, wonderful, and vital part of any successful relationship. The deep and fulfilling joy that two people experience as they fall in love is the strong foundation that all LTLRs need to build upon for the future. The bonding and commitment that Sweet Symbiosis provides is absolutely necessary for any couple to have a chance of weathering the inevitable storms that hit later in the life of the LTLR. Challenges do lie ahead, starting with stage 2.

Stage 2: Soured Symbiosis

The honeymoon never lasts forever. No Long-Term Love Relationship is able to perpetually maintain itself in the blissfulness of Sweet Symbiosis. It's sad, but true. There's a common misconception in our culture that you should be able to make the magic of stage 1 last throughout your LTLR and if it doesn't, then something must be wrong with you, your partner, or your relationship. Some people go from partner to partner, leaving each one as soon as the magic starts fading, thinking that maybe the next person will be the one that provides that blind bliss forever. Some couples come to us wanting help recapturing the magic of stage 1 so they can live in the honeymoon till death do they part.

But that is an unrealistic goal, and we tell them so. The wonderful sweet symbiosis of stage 1 is unsustainable for all couples, no matter how well matched. Why? Because even with "a match made in heaven," problems inevitably emerge between two people in love. Hurts and disappointments occur. You find traits, interests, and behaviors in your partner that you wish were different, parts of him that you don't like. Does that mean that all of a sudden you don't love him anymore? Of course not, but once you and he start noticing these things about the other, love is no longer blind.

So the emergence of the awareness of issues and differences marks the beginning of stage 2, what we call Soured Symbiosis. This is where many couples get stuck in the growth and development of their LTLR. Most couples that come to see us are deep in Soured Symbiosis and are unable to find their way out of it.

There is one very simple reason for this. Many, if not most, of us never learned how to develop good, healthy emotional intimacy with another person. Most of us never learned how to really be close to another person, not only in regard to positive, warm, and loving feelings but also in regard to negative, painful, and angry feelings.

Now most of us have at least some ability to be loving with another person and to express and share these emotions in a way that feels good to our partner. But it is much more difficult and much rarer for a person to be good at dealing with their hurts, disappointments, and angers with their partner in a healthy way. And it is rarer still for a person to be good at this as well as being good at dealing with her partner's negative feelings toward her.

That is why when the honeymoon is over and differences start to emerge between two people in love, their LTLR will run aground on the treacherous rocks of Soured Symbiosis. This stage is called Soured Symbiosis because it is defined by the hard feelings that conflict generates once Sweet Symbiosis starts to fade.

However, it is very important to realize that while this stage in LTLRs can be difficult and painful, it is also healthy and normal. In fact, it's a key transitional period. How a couple deals with Soured Symbiosis determines whether an LTLR is going to last and thrive for the long run.

You see, since the bliss of Sweet Symbiosis cannot last forever, couples need to learn to make adjustments and grow together so that the love and intimacy between them can flourish. Whereas blind love drove the relationship in stage 1, eyes-open love is needed in stage 2 to keep the LTLR moving ahead.

This is where emotional intimacy comes in. It is the fuel that gets couples through the second stage of their LTLR.

Now by "emotional intimacy" we don't mean that in order for couples to grow they have to talk about their innermost feelings all the time. What we mean here is that couples must get good at communicating, at dealing with their feelings, good and bad. And communication isn't only about talking. It's also about acting, about how you treat each other, about doing and saying things that make each other feel loved, respected, and appreciated.

Most often the problems arise not in making your partner feel loved, but in dealing with him when differences and conflicts occur. Couples get into trouble here by settling into one of two maladaptive patterns for dealing with conflicts. We mentioned these conflict styles, Hostile Dependent and Conflict Avoidant, earlier, and will discuss them in more detail in chapter 6. Understanding which one your relationship falls into is essential in moving past Soured Symbiosis to stage 3.

Stage 3: Differentiation

This is the homestretch for every Long-Term Love Relationship. Entering stage 3 means that your LTLR has a very good chance of thriving and lasting for a long time.

That's because this phase indicates that you've begun to build into your LTLR the ability to deal well with your differences. It signifies that you're developing the true emotional intimacy that will power fulfillment in your relationship.

"Differentiation" is a fancy word to describe the stage when a couple is strong enough in their love that they can successfully discuss and deal with the conflict between them. So it's about loving and enjoying each other, and also about being able to work well together when you're not so happy with each other. It's about soaking up the good times with each other, making wonderful memories, and it's about confronting, dealing with, and putting aside the bad times.

The hallmark of stage 3 is the ability of both partners to deal with conflict well. Stage 3 couples don't slip into Hostile Dependent or Conflict Avoidant patterns, but work to handle conflicts in a healthy way. We'll get into how you do this in detail in chapter 6, but for now suffice it to say that this is all about getting good at both speaking up and at listening up. That means expressing who you are and what you're feeling in a nonaggressive way, and hearing your partner when he does the same without taking it personally and getting defensive.

A pivotal step in achieving Differentiation is both partners being willing to take responsibility for their part in the problems in the relationship and then sincerely working on making necessary changes in themselves or in their behavior. It is only when each of you is willing to do this that you can deal with conflict well. Only when you're willing to admit that you've made a mistake, that you're not perfect, can you be a good partner. Only when both of you have the strength and self-confidence to do this can you meet each other halfway and join hands in building a great LTLR. It's then that your relationship gets to the ultimate stage of LTLR development.

Stage 4: Synergy

This is the gravy. Stage 4 is where truly happy couples who have been together for years are. You know, the couples whose happiness and love you've envied? They've achieved the final stage of LTLR growth, Synergy. They've weathered the storms, navigated around the shoals of Soured Symbiosis, and come through the stronger for it. They've gone through changes and conflicts, dealt with them, and grown closer as a result.

That's one of the great things about conflict in LTLRs. When done well, conflict is *the* most powerful means there is to build love relationship strength. Meeting disagreements head on, working through them, and resolving them builds confidence in the relationship and in each other. This increases the intimacy in the relationship. And it grows the love, affection, and appreciation that you have for each other.

In stage 4, a couple has solidified the gains they made in achieving Differentiation. Dealing with conflict well is now second nature to them. They've developed the strength in their LTLR to deal with difficult times and the resiliency to rebound from the stresses and traumas that life can bring. They're good at loving each other, at showing their love in ways that touch them both. Each partner knows who they are (chapter 5) and is good at sharing their self with their life partner. Synergy is the mature flowering of love, what we all yearn for in our love relationship.

Regressing in the Face of Stress

One final note about the developmental model of Long-Term Love Relationships: the process of relationship growth doesn't only move in a forward direction. This is a major difference between how individuals and LTLRs grow. No adult can truly become a child again (of course, we can act like one, though!), but an "adult" LTLR can.

During times of high stress, couples that have reached stage 3 or even stage 4 may regress to the earlier, less mature functioning of stage 2. When any of us is under enough strain, we will become less patient, less understanding, more self-absorbed, and more irritable. These stress reactions can then cause us to engage in the toxic conflict patterns of Soured Symbiosis.

Does that mean we're back to square one in our LTLR? Does that mean we've lost all the gains and happiness and security we worked so hard to attain? Not at all. Usually when the source of the stress that caused the regression is gone, the higher, more mature level of LTLR functioning will return.

This bidirectional nature of LTLR development is quite common in psychological growth processes. For individuals as well as couples, taking steps backward at times is neither unusual nor does it need to be permanent. The most important thing to remember is that as long as you and your partner persevere and keep working at your relationship, nothing will be able to stop your eventual progress forward.

WHY HE BETRAYED YOU WHEN HE DID

Where every LTLR is at any given time, including yours, can be pinpointed within these four developmental stages. You may have already recognized for yourself where your LTLR is. But even if you haven't, we have.

Yep, we know exactly where you and your partner are in the developmental model. That's because, as we mentioned at the beginning of this chapter, infidelities always happen at the same point in a love relationship's development: stage 2, Soured Symbiosis.

Your partner betrayed you now because there's been a challenge to the intimacy in your LTLR and the two of you haven't mastered the difficulties. Again, this does not mean that the infidelity is your fault. It was your partner's choice. No matter what's been going on in the relationship, he didn't have to make that choice.

But somehow the two of you must have gotten yourselves into either the Hostile Dependent or the Conflict Avoidant process pattern, and this weakened your bond. He reacted by engaging in an infidelity. No matter what the circumstances surrounding the infidelity, no matter what reasons he may give you for why he did it, it always comes back to the two of you being stuck in Soured Symbiosis. The resulting loss of emotional intimacy created an opening, a vulnerability to infidelity.

Sometimes, unfortunately, the betrayed partner can think that the relationship is still in Sweet Symbiosis only to be devastated by her partner's unfaithfulness. This happens when her partner is in some ways quite psychologically immature; he is so afraid of intimacy that he sabotages the love relationship with an infidelity, a cowardly and destructive means of escape (see chapter 9).

But most often infidelities occur when the toxic patterns of dealing with conflict have been going on for a while. This is likely the case with you and your partner; you've been stuck in Soured Symbiosis for some time. Differences, conflicts, hurts, disappointments, and resentments have arisen and the two of you have either been ignoring them or hurting each other further by having nasty fights about them.

You may not have been aware of how unhappy your partner was. And even he may not have been aware of these feelings. Emotional self-awareness and emotional self-disclosure are not strong suits for most guys.

And how aware have you been of your own hurts and disappointments? If you were quite aware of them, you didn't find a way to effectively deal with them. If you weren't very aware of them, then that is a whole other problem (that we'll deal with in the next chapter). Either way, your partner's infidelity happened now because your LTLR has stopped growing.

And instead of facing this head-on, your partner chose to run to another woman. He did that now because on some level he feared that your relationship would never be good again, that it would never be like he, and you, want it to be. And he's got a right to have that fear. But the choice he made lacked integrity.

Your LTLR has been facing the test of the Soured Symbiosis stage. You and your partner failed. And you got hurt, badly. But that doesn't mean all is lost.

SOURED SYMBIOSIS IN OUR FOUR COUPLES

Each of the couples has sought help because they are struggling to regain confidence in their relationship. Despite the apparent differences in the couples, including the length of their relationships and their presenting problems—infidelity, financial disagreements, constant arguing, and/or growing dissatisfactions—each couple is struggling with Soured Symbiosis and needs assistance to arrive at the stability of the next stage of relationship growth, the Differentiation stage.

■ Gracie and Jake: An Infidelity of Fear

Gracie and Jake had a very positive period of Sweet Symbiosis. Gracie loved the attention she received from Jake and the way he made her feel whole, and he enjoyed her appreciation of him. Gracie liked their marriage yet often found herself yearning to stand out and be noticed by other men.

Gracie did not view this need as a threat to her marriage. She liked to flirt and convinced herself that it was harmless. Most of the time she avoided the nagging disappointment that being Jake's wife was not enough to make her feel completely satisfied. The vague and growing presence of this dissatisfaction signaled that Gracie had moved from the enveloping optimism of Sweet Symbiosis to the contrasting reality of Soured Symbiosis.

Jake enjoyed his wife's beauty and was not threatened by the interest that men paid her. He trusted her and even was proud of the fact that men noticed her. He had no recognition of her disappointments in their relationship. He was still enjoying the benefits of Sweet Symbiosis.

Gracie does not recognize that her desire for the attention of other men is an indication of some personal or relationship dissatisfaction, so she cannot anticipate the road that she is traveling on. Her unspoken disappointment in her marriage places her on a path that leads her to feel more and more separate from her husband and this contributes to her decision to be unfaithful.

If Gracie saw that her need for other men's attention was a problem for her marriage, then she could do things differently. One choice would be to determine the source of this dissatisfaction; is it primarily about herself or does it come from something missing in her LTLR?

Unbeknownst to them, Gracie and Jake have moved from Sweet Symbiosis to Soured Symbiosis. For Gracie, Soured Symbiosis represents a change in her sense of self in the relationship and the reappearance of her unresolved sense of personal satisfaction. As her desire for the attention of other men goes unexamined, it will begin to dictate the choices she makes both within and outside of her marriage. She tells herself that Jake cannot meet all her needs, and she builds the justification in her mind for an infidelity.

■ Samantha and Paul: An Infidelity of Loneliness

Samantha and Paul both enjoyed the early parts of their relationship. They each commented on how the other represented what they had always looked for in a mate. However, as the relationship grew, Samantha and Paul often disagreed about how to spend money. Paul wanted a budget so they could anticipate their expenses while Samantha enjoyed spur-of-the-moment purchases and found a budget restrictive. At first, they usually arrived at compromises that both of them could live with; however, over time Samantha began to view Paul as financially controlling while Paul viewed Samantha as passive-aggressive with money issues as well as a spendthrift.

These financial differences began to push Paul and Samantha out of the comfort of Sweet Symbiosis into the tension of Soured Symbiosis. Both felt the shift, yet neither of them knew how to talk about it. Instead, they each tried to convince the other of the legitimacy of their view or tried to get the other to compromise. Despite any temporary solutions they would agree to, they were both beginning to subtly experience discomfort and growing pains in their relationship. It was in this context of growing differences, the inability to resolve differences, and increased dissatisfaction that Paul began his affair with a woman from work.

■ Amy and Lewis: An Infidelity of Anger

Amy and Lewis experienced a short but intense period of Sweet Symbiosis during their early courtship. As they started to run into conflict, neither of them wanted to admit their fears and uncertainties about the stability and strength of the relationship. They would choose to believe that the other person would change over time and then the relationship would be calm and loving. Only at their worst moments of anger or of feeling victimized by the other did they acknowledge how soured their relationship had become. And even then, they were only able to see the role that the other played in their problems. Unfortunately for them, Soured Symbiosis arrived early in the relationship.

With only short periods of closeness and the relationship becoming less predictable, Lewis began to believe that Amy was blaming him. He felt victimized and angry. The two of them would argue, but were unable to discuss their hurts and disappointments constructively. Lewis did not know how to console himself when he felt shut off from Amy. Amy, for her part, kept convincing herself that Lewis would change and tried hard to let go of her anger and disappointment. Their inability to bridge their differences led Lewis to seek solace from others. He felt that this was justified by Amy's harsh treatment of him.

■ Cindy and Scott: Growing Pains Without Infidelity

As Cindy and Scott dated, they enjoyed and appreciated the commonalities of their cultural backgrounds. They found that they had similar senses of humor and points of reference. Their Sweet

Symbiosis lasted for more than a year as their mutual attraction fueled their blind and wonderful new love.

The first signs of their differences came as they met one another's parents. Cindy was attracted to Scott's family's ethnic background, yet she found them to be close-minded and dependent in their interactions with one another. She would verbalize her frustrations to Scott and was disappointed when he was unable or unwilling to see her point of view.

Scott enjoyed Cindy's enthusiasm but found himself feeling annoyed with her expectation that he or his family act differently. "After all," he thought, "I've had to live with them this way my whole life. Why should they have to be different for her?" Instead of verbalizing this, he found himself avoiding the discussions with Cindy, or cutting them short. At his worst moments, he would explode at her and accuse her of being critical and demanding. Over time he also came to resent her family as he believed she perceived it as being superior to his.

Cindy and Scott have moved from the sweet start to their relationship into the reality of their differences. They know that the honeymoon is over, but they do not yet have a way to discuss their disappointments without blaming the other. Therefore, they vacillate between feeling optimistic about their relationship and experiencing frustration and hurt.

What These Four Couples Teach You

As you have read, each of these couples started out with the best of intentions and a desire to succeed in their relationship; however, when the inevitable differences appeared, each was limited in their ability to face the challenges and move their relationship from the unstable stage of Soured Symbiosis to the more solid and satisfying stage of Differentiation.

The challenge for Gracie and Jake came from Gracie's vague sense of dissatisfaction in the relationship and her unwillingness to acknowledge this feeling and its effect on her view of Jake and herself. Gracie's growing dissatisfaction and unexpressed desire for more from Jake destabilize what was the Sweet (and satisfying) Symbiosis between them. Without recognizing what she is feeling,

Gracie cannot do anything to diminish her dissatisfaction and its growing presence in her relationship. Her insecurities coupled with her low Self-Intimacy have formed a potent mix that puts her LTLR at risk for infidelity.

Paul and Samantha's disagreements about money expose the difficult differences between them. They have tried to bridge their differences but have not been able to arrive at a mutual solution. Consequently, distance is growing between them that will extend beyond financial concerns and begin to create a chasm in their sense of closeness, intimacy, and relationship confidence. This distance will eventually allow a sense of loneliness to take root, which will develop into a potential for an infidelity.

Amy and Lewis discovered their problems earlier perhaps than the other three couples and consequently, they have less resiliency in their relationship. The continued disappointments and lack of resolution make them vulnerable to overreact to differences with anger and accusations. Each of them has become inflexible in the relationship and while both want the relationship to endure, neither knows how to effectively reconcile their differences and disappointments. As this couple continues to confront problems, they get stuck in a pattern of either overt or "underground" arguing that results in added destruction to the fabric of the relationship and creates ground for an infidelity to occur, bolstered by feelings of anger and self-justification.

Cindy and Scott encountered their differences gradually as their relationship evolved. Consequently, they have more goodwill in their relationship that helps them when they face the disappointments and enter Soured Symbiosis. They have resiliency in their relationship peppered with their disappointments. They try to talk and work toward resolution, but often feel stymied. Their struggles result in both positive and negative feelings about the other, yet their commitment to the relationship remains strong. What does this couple have that the other three lack? At this point, we might answer that they do not yet have a grooved pattern of responding to conflict and neither has begun to feel significantly separate from the other—yet they have clearly entered Soured Symbiosis.

Inevitable growth is what is compelling these couples to move from the relationship stage of Sweet Symbiosis to Soured Symbiosis. Each person now has to face the reality that relationships include disappointments.

Disappointments do not end a relationship or single-handedly lead to infidelity. It is when we do not notice or value our experience of dissatisfaction that we start off on the slippery slope toward infidelity. Gracie, Paul, and Lewis are less capable of tolerating the disappointment that they are experiencing and so look outside the relationship.

REBOUNDING FROM INFIDELITY

You and your partner can rebound from this—yes, even from this devastating infidelity. Remember, all couples go through the trials of Soured Symbiosis. All couples struggle with it. All couples hurt each other at this stage, all disappoint each other at this stage, and all have doubts whether they can make it through this stage. Some never do. Some partners fail and have an infidelity. But some of those couples shattered by infidelity are able to come back from it stronger. Read on and we'll get you started on doing just that.

Chapter Review

What Stage Is Your Relationship in Presently?

1. *Sweet Symbiosis:* The early part of the relationship characterized by the similarities between the two of you. This is the honeymoon during which you lay the foundation for your affection and investment in one another. It usually lasts around eighteen months.

2. *Soured Symbiosis:* This change is marked by the emerging awareness of the differences between the

two of you and your experience of disappointment or disenchantment. This is normal and expected and requires that the two of you face these experiences and feelings directly with one another or the beginnings of relationship problems are laid.

3. *Differentiation:* Each of you begins to regain your separate sense of self and is able to accept the partner for who s/he is—both strengths and weaknesses. In the face of your differences, you are able to respect both your viewpoint and that of your partner.

4. *Synergy:* The relationship evolves to a stage where you are each able to move back and forth between working for your own best interests and those of the relationship.

Under stress, all relationships can regress to Soured Symbiosis. But as the couple deals with the stress, the relationship can return to the previous higher level of functioning.

- Where is your relationship currently?

- Consider the length of time your relationship was in Sweet Symbiosis.

- Ask yourself what heralded for you the beginning of Soured Symbiosis.

- Consider how you have dealt with the disappointment of Soured Symbiosis; did you ignore it, minimize it, or criticize your partner?

- How did you try to bring up your disappointments?

- What did you let stop you when you were trying to discuss them?

- ■ Try to pinpoint if there have been times when
  your relationship has successfully navigated
  disappointments.

The answers to these questions will help you to understand where your relationship is today and how, for you, it arrived there. If your partner is reading the book, have him answer these questions. Then, using the I-to-I tool in chapter 6, share your answers with your partner.

The answer to the last point can assist you in determining what ways or skills you have successfully used in the past to get through difficulties. Examine what they were and determine if they've stopped working. If so, why? If your old coping skills and negotiating mechanisms no longer function, it could indicate that your relationship has been going through a period of growth, unbeknownst to either of you.

chapter 4

the three intimacies: the building blocks of a relationship

The meeting of two personalities is like the contact of two chemical substances: if there is any reaction, both are transformed. —Carl Jung

Age does not protect you from love, but love to some extent protects you from age. —Jeanne Moreau

What makes long-term love relationships tick? What makes the good ones work and the not-so-good ones fail? Why are some people so good at love while others can't seem to make a go of it?

How do you answer these questions? Poets, playwrights, and philosophers have wrestled with such mysteries for ages. Does love conquer all? Or is the answer something less romantic than that: is compromise the key?

What is the secret to LTLR success?

This is the question that we have focused on in our work as couples therapists. The countless couples in crisis who have come to us for help have shown that no, love is not enough, and it does not conquer all. And no, compromise is not the secret to success.

Both love and compromise are necessary for a relationship to flourish, but neither is sufficient to ensure LTLR success.

THE THREE INTIMACIES

We've found that the key factor enabling two people to be happy together for the long term is the ability to be intimate. Intimacy is the secret ingredient that successfully powers a couple through the developmental stages of LTLRs. So the recipe for true LTLR happiness is a very simple one: a generous dollop of love sprinkled with a healthy helping of intimacy.

But what do we mean when we talk about intimacy? Well, we're not simply referring to a sense of closeness and we're not just talking about great sex. Both are important but they are both the results of intimacy, not its essence.

Successful LTLRs rely on three types of intimacy: Self-Intimacy, Conflict Intimacy, and Affection Intimacy. Together, these intimacies allow you to share who you are with your partner, to fight well with your partner, and to be loving with your partner. We'll describe each of the intimacies in detail in the following chapters.

Your Best Defense Against Infidelity

If you and your partner are good at the three intimacies, the love between you will thrive over time instead of wither with each passing year. The three intimacies enable a couple to move through the stages of love, especially through Soured Symbiosis, so that their relationship is no longer fertile ground for infidelity.

Understanding and developing your strength in each of the intimacies is the most powerful way for you to become good at long-term love. And if your partner joins you in working on the three intimacies, there is very little that can stand in the way of the two of you loving and growing together. Becoming strong in the three intimacies is your relationship's best defense against future infidelity, and a very, very potent defense it is.

Building Blocks

There are a few things for you to understand before we get started helping you construct this defense. We talk of the three intimacies as building blocks because we think of them as the basis of a healthy relationship. Not only that, but the three intimacies build upon each other.

Think of them as the levels of a multistory house. The foundation of the house rests upon Self-Intimacy. Only after you have built this solid foundation of self-knowledge can you add the first story, Conflict Intimacy. And only after you've developed a first floor of fighting well can you add the second floor, Affection Intimacy, the ability to love each other well.

Through all of these levels, you and your partner's emotions remain central in the development of true intimacy. Emotions are the most intimate part of ourselves that we can share with another human being. Your ability to develop your awareness of your own emotions, as well as your ability to share both positive, loving emotions and negative, angry ones, will determine your capacity to love well and be loved well.

So the key to success in long-term love relationships is how well two partners deal with their emotions, both within themselves and between them. The secret to making sure that your LTLR is not fertile ground for another infidelity isn't about removing stresses from your relationship, but about how you deal with the stresses.

Many couples who are struggling with infidelity come to us and the betrayed partner can't stop trying to figure out the reason for her partner's betrayal. Was it because he lost his job? Is he going through a midlife crisis? Am I not attractive enough? Was the sex not good enough? Was it not often enough? Was it financial stress? We have found that none of these factors are ever the root cause. Infidelity doesn't happen because of any one stressor. Infidelities, as well as LTLR failure, only occur in response to not dealing with the stresses of life effectively.

Every LTLR is faced with troubles and crises. Some of them are triggered by a problem within one of the partners, like low self-esteem or a fear of intimacy. Others are triggered by problems between the partners, like resentments and unresolved hurts and disappointments. Some are triggered by external events, like the loss of a job or, god forbid, the death of a child. But it is how the two partners deal with these issues, not the issues themselves, that determine whether one or even both partners will choose the path of infidelity.

That's where the three intimacies come in. Developing skill in these intimacies empowers a couple to deal well with any stresses. In fact, instead of being weakened by trials and tribulations, the Long-Term Love Relationship of a couple that is good at the three intimacies is actually strengthened by dealing with challenges and crises together. Their bond, forged by fire, becomes even tighter.

Chapter Review

Review the definitions of each of the three intimacies and determine how intimate you are in each one. You can also consider where your partner is, but realize that the only person you can change is yourself, so focus mostly on your intimacy capacity.

The Three Intimacies

1. *Self-Intimacy:* The moment-to-moment awareness of one's feelings, thoughts, and needs as well as the willingness to acknowledge and own these to oneself and with one's partner. The tool we use to develop Self-Intimacy is the Emotional Self-Awareness (ESA) Exercise.

2. *Conflict Intimacy:* The ability to acknowledge and share your feelings, thoughts, and needs with your partner, especially difficult and negative ones. Conflict Intimacy also involves being able to hear and accept the same from your partner, as well as remaining involved in difficult conversations until a

mutually agreed upon resolution is reached. The tool for Conflict Intimacy is the Initiator-to-Inquirer, the I-to-I.

3. *Affection Intimacy:* The ability to express your love and caring for a partner through actions, words, and physical means. We define four types of Affection Intimacy:

    a. *Verbal Affection Intimacy:* using words to express caring

    b. *Actions Affection Intimacy:* taking actions to express caring

    c. *Sexual Affection Intimacy:* sexuality as an expression of caring

    d. *Nonsexual Physical Affection Intimacy:* touches, rubs, hand holding, etc., to express caring

As you determine which of the three intimacies you can benefit from developing, read ahead to chapters 5 through 7 to learn the specific skills that will improve your Self-Intimacy, Conflict Intimacy, and Affection Intimacy.

chapter 5

self-intimacy: the bedrock of the relationship

*One learns through the heart, not the eyes
or the intellect.* —Mark Twain

Never let anyone, including yourself, convince you that you drove your man into another woman's arms. That is never, ever true. We don't care what's been going on in your relationship, we don't care what kind of partner you've been to him—you didn't make him do it. It was his choice and he needs to take responsibility for it.

Taking responsibility for the actions of another person is a common mistake. In analyzing an LTLR in crisis, many couples and even some couples therapists simply assume that infidelity, as well as any other problems in the relationship, is caused by flaws between the two partners. Quite often the interpersonal relationship is not the actual root of the problem; frequently it lies in one partner's relationship with his or her self.

THE IMPORTANCE OF SELF-INTIMACY

There's no denying that it is difficult to have a good love relationship with someone else if you don't have a good love relationship with yourself. Put another way, it's hard to be intimate with your partner if you are not intimate with yourself. That is why Self-Intimacy is so essential and why it is the foundation of a healthy LTLR.

Without Self-Intimacy (SI), your relationship is not on solid ground; it is vulnerable to infidelity. The common denominator that we find in people who are unfaithful is low SI. Infidelities are committed by people from all walks of life: men, women, old, young, rich, poor, educated, uneducated, and so on. But the one thing we find in all of them is limited Self-Intimacy.

Self-Intimacy Defined

So what is Self-Intimacy, exactly? We've coined this term to refer to your ability to know what's going on within yourself, and based on that knowledge, act in ways that take good care of yourself. We're not talking about being self-centered or selfish, but about looking after yourself. None of us can do a good job of that unless we first know who we are, and understand what we're thinking, wanting, and feeling.

The Primacy of Your Emotions

Of those three aspects of self (thinking, wanting, and feeling), becoming aware of what you are feeling is by far the most important in developing Self-Intimacy.

Think of your emotions as messages from your true self, your soul, your inner being. These messages tell you how you're doing keeping your life on a path that is healthy or righteous for you. Positive emotions usually tell you that whatever is going on is good for you, that it is something to appreciate and keep in your life. Negative emotions are a tap on the shoulder telling you that there is some problem in your life and that you need to pay attention to it.

Self-Intimacy and Gender

Now, it's important to see that SI isn't just about being emotionally self-aware. It's also about using that emotional self-awareness to take effective action that will keep your life on track.

Women are commonly seen as more emotionally self-aware than men. In many, if not most, cultures men are trained through norms and mores to focus more on their thoughts than on their feelings, so both their awareness of and their expression of emotions tend not to be as good as that of women.

However, in many cultures women are taught through negative reinforcement that it's not "appropriate" or "ladylike" for them to stand up for themselves. So we have found that neither gender has a corner on SI. Women tend to be better at being aware of their emotions, while men are often better at taking effective action in standing up for themselves.

Self-Intimacy and Your Partner

But how does SI enter into what's happened in your relationship? Your partner is or has been unfaithful to you; what does SI have to do with that? Well, as we mentioned, most people who are unfaithful have low SI. That is, either they are not very aware of their emotions, especially their negative emotions; they are not very good at addressing the problems their negative emotions are pointing out to them; or both. Are you seeing your partner here?

When we talk about negative emotions, we're referring to fear, loneliness, anger, hurt, disappointment, and sadness. The problem isn't that your partner has been feeling these things, but how he did or, more accurately, didn't deal with them. His SI must not be high enough for him to both be aware of these emotions and to take healthy action to deal with the problems that cause them. What happened is what always happens when any of us don't pay attention to our emotions: instead of him being in control of them, they took control of him. And so he betrayed you.

Self-Intimacy and You

But what about your level of SI? Does that have anything to do with what's happened? Could problems in your level of SI have contributed to your partner betraying you? Absolutely not; that was his choice and his choice alone. You could be the most self-intimate person on earth and he could still have betrayed you.

So is SI important for you at all? Yes. There's no question about it, for two main reasons. First, as you work to recover from the infidelity and to heal the relationship with your partner, the more self-intimate you are, the more intimate you will be able to be with him. The more you know yourself, the more of yourself you will be able to share with him, which will go a long way toward rebuilding the closeness in the relationship.

Second, the more you develop your SI, the more sensitive you will be in the future to indications that your LTLR is straying into infidelity-vulnerable territory. Your heightened Self-Intimacy will be an early warning system, alerting you to when there are unresolved issues in your LTLR. Because you will be attuned to your emotions, you'll be aware when something is wrong. And, instead of dismissing this feeling, talking yourself out of it, or ignoring it, you'll pay attention and bring it up with your partner.

THE EMOTIONAL SELF-AWARENESS (ESA) EXERCISE

So then the question becomes, how do you and your partner each work on your Self-Intimacy? Years ago, we developed a simple three-step exercise to do just that.

Ask yourself three questions:

1. What emotion(s) am I feeling right now?

2. What situation or perception of mine is causing me to feel this emotion(s)?

3. What, if anything, can I do about this causal situation to take good care of myself?

For example, I'm feeling hurt and angry (#1) because when I left the house this morning my wife didn't kiss me good-bye (#2). In response to this I could call her up and yell at her, give her the cold shoulder when I get home, or call her to tell her what I'm feeling (#3). Obviously the last idea is the healthiest one.

Getting good at answering these three questions and then taking action based on the answer to question number 3 will give you unbelievable control over your life. You will become the captain of your ship. We have found that this simple exercise is the single most powerful tool we can give people. Those that really practice the ESA exercise are amazed at the dramatic improvement it makes in their emotional well-being and their quality of life in general.

KEYS FOR ESA SUCCESS

There are a few keys to getting good at the ESA exercise.

A Little Time Every Day

Just like lifting weights, the more times you do this exercise, the stronger you will become. Continuing with the bodybuilding analogy, the secret here is lots of repetitions with light weights. That is, do the ESA two or three times a day, but not for very long each time. Only spend a minute or two on it, otherwise it will become too burdensome and you'll stop doing it.

Remember to Do It

Over the many years in which we've given our clients the task of doing the ESA exercise, we've found that oftentimes they have trouble remembering to do it. Focusing on our internal emotional world runs counter to how we are trained in Western society, particularly for men. We tend to be so externally focused; when we are focused internally, it is almost always on our thoughts.

One of the first clients we assigned the exercise to was a man who just could not remember to check in with his feelings. So we told him to tie the exercise to something he did every day, a few times a day, that didn't require much concentration, like brushing his teeth, washing the dishes, and so on. He was to use this everyday activity as a reminder to do the exercise. Well, he came back to the office a week later and with a sheepish grin stated that he was doing the exercise great now: he just did it whenever he went to the bathroom and called it Piss Therapy! If you find that you have trouble remembering to do the ESA exercise, take a lesson from this client: develop your own memory device, your own Piss Therapy.

Be Specific

A common mistake is to answer question number 1 with thoughts instead of real feelings, like, "I'm feeling that it was a mistake to take revenge on my partner for being unfaithful to me by destroying his most prized possessions." That isn't a feeling just because you put the word "feeling" in front of it. A better description would be: "I'm feeling so incredibly hurt and enraged that my partner betrayed me with another woman." Try to name specific feelings like hurt, sad, angry, disappointed, jealous, afraid, happy, peaceful, excited, and so on.

Achieving Awareness

There's one last key to having success with the ESA exercise. When first trying it, some people, most often men, have trouble answering question number 1. They'll come back to us and say, "I don't have any feelings." They aren't able to achieve awareness of their emotions when doing the exercise. We tell them that this isn't because the feelings aren't there. We all have feelings all the time. You've heard the phrase "stream of consciousness." Well, think of your emotional life as a stream of affect, of emotion. It's always flowing. You just have to develop the ability to dip your toe in and test the waters. Some of us are just not very good at this. The only time we're aware of emotions is when they're so strong they practically hit us in the face.

But that's the power of the ESA exercise. If you do it two to three times a day for the next ninety days, you will become exquisitely aware of your emotions when you're having them. Your emotional awareness will become second nature. Eventually, you won't have to consciously do the exercise; you'll just start finding that you're aware of what you're feeling and you'll know what it is.

But if you find that you know you're feeling something and can't quite figure out what it is, use the list of emotions in appendix D as a checklist. Run through it and see which emotion(s) best fits what you are experiencing.

As you get better at identifying what you are feeling, don't be surprised when you have more than one emotion about an experience. And on top of that, sometimes these various feelings may seem to be contradictory. Don't worry, there's nothing wrong with you; this is not unusual. While it's natural for you to feel great anger toward your partner for the betrayal, you are likely to also still feel love for him at times, along with deep hurt, sadness, fear, need, desperation, and revenge.

MAKE YOUR EMOTIONAL WORLD A PRIORITY

In our modern world, a very high premium is placed on intellectual strength, and indeed, it is important. However, we have found in our work helping people find happiness and fulfillment in their LTLRs that developing a connection between the heart and the mind is much more important than intellectual smarts.

The primary cause of the high divorce rate in our society is the failure to recognize the primacy of emotions in our personal lives. That is why so many LTLRs fail to fulfill their promise and end in estrangement, because one or both partners never learned the importance of being emotionally self-aware. Never having developed the ability to be self-intimate, they were hamstrung in the ability to be intimate with a partner.

Without that ability, when the going gets tough in an LTLR, when Sweet Symbiosis turns into Soured Symbiosis, partners don't know how to deal with it and the relationship starts to founder. That's when disappointments and resentments start to build. That's when distance between partners is created. That's when infidelities happen.

But you have a great chance of avoiding this path if you make your emotions a priority, if both you and your partner develop Self-Intimacy.

YOU AND YOUR PARTNER'S COMMITMENT TO SELF-INTIMACY

But what if your partner isn't motivated to work on his own SI while you work on yours? What if he gives a halfhearted effort and doesn't stick with the ESA exercise? Does it make any sense for you to persevere in developing your SI? Absolutely it does. The more self-intimate you are, the clearer you can see your choices and your part in your LTLR, and the more able you are to take good care of yourself in the relationship.

The more Self-Intimacy you have, the smarter you will be in your LTLR. You'll know what feels right and what feels wrong. You'll be able to take effective action in defense of the relationship, guiding your LTLR back on course when it gets off track. And you'll know if and when it's time to give up and end the relationship.

But it's a bad sign if your partner refuses to work on SI. It may indicate that he's not committed to healing and growing your LTLR. If that's the case, you need to assess whether he's the right partner for you. You need someone who will meet you halfway, who will work on your LTLR as hard as you will, and someone to whom your relationship is as important as it is to you. You deserve no less. Without such real dedication, you are unlikely to realize your dreams for your LTLR with him. Your relationship will continue to be infidelity vulnerable.

You Have the Power

Whether or not your partner joins you in this work, your ability to develop Self-Intimacy is totally within your power. Working on your Self-Intimacy is a win-win situation. Becoming more self-intimate means you'll start taking better care of yourself, and this will build respect and love for yourself. As you learn how to keep your life on a healthy path, you'll become a more positive, happy person.

Your life path may include the partner who has been unfaithful to you. It may not. But if it does, it will be for the right reasons—because you and he are both committed to your love and to each other, because both of you are doing whatever you can to heal from the injury of the infidelity and rebuild your LTLR.

So Self-Intimacy is the bedrock, the first building block of your LTLR house. Your partner's infidelity is like an earthquake rocking the house. With the solid foundation that Self-Intimacy affords, your LTLR can weather the trauma. Without it, your relationship will likely be razed.

SELF-INTIMACY IN PRACTICE

To bring Self-Intimacy into sharper focus, let's look at how SI affected the relationships of two of your companion couples.

■ Gracie and Jake: An Infidelity of Fear

Gracie has begun to feel dissatisfied with aspects of family life. She finds herself wanting to be noticed for her own merits rather than as a wife or parent. She is unaware of the source of these feelings and even dismisses their presence and any importance they may have. Consequently, she finds herself "going through the motions" with Jake at home as they deal with day-to-day events and even feeling bored at some family functions. In contrast, she finds herself looking forward to work where she is noticed for her own contributions and is enlivened in social settings.

Because she minimizes her feelings of dissatisfaction, she also avoids acknowledging her growing feelings of disappointment and occasional resentments toward Jake.

Before Jake learned of her infidelities, Gracie sought counseling for herself after years of infidelities and flirtations. In the course of therapy she became more willing to examine the array of feelings she had. She discovered that she often felt bored, unimportant, jealous, and competitive. She was surprised at the feelings and struggled with wanting to deny them. She had to fight her desire to believe that her dissatisfaction in her marriage was to be expected and begin to acknowledge that her feelings were having a significant effect on her behavior both toward Jake and other men.

Until Gracie was willing to pay attention to her emotions and the influence they had over her actions, she had few choices. She had learned to deal with her infidelities by guilting herself into stopping her affairs, but the effectiveness of that strategy was short-lived. Then she would rationalize to herself that her infidelities were not hurting Jake and continue to live her dual lives.

As Gracie became more comfortable recognizing her feelings—both positive and negative—she saw how powerful they were. She realized that acknowledging her feelings gave her more viable choices. She continued practicing the Emotional Self-Awareness Exercise and gained confidence that trusting her feelings was in her best interest. Over time, she began to talk with Jake about some of her dissatisfactions with the marriage. While this was not yet a solution to her marital difficulties and pattern of infidelities, it was a beginning. For the first time in many years she saw a way to understand what had been motivating her.

Jake at this point is not aware of his wife's infidelities. However, he has noticed that Gracie often seems distracted, disinterested, and/or preoccupied. Unfortunately, Jake, like Gracie, is not in touch with nor comfortable with many of his feelings. As long as he and Gracie are not in an argument he believes that everything is fine between them.

Jake's limited Self-Intimacy hamstrings him both personally and in the marriage. Because he is uncomfortable acknowledging his feelings, especially negative or problematic ones, it is impossible for him to help Gracie understand and talk about her distractedness and to learn how to deal with his own negative feelings. When he finds out about Gracie's infidelity, the sheer power of the feelings will be uncomfortable for him. His discomfort and limited experience with feelings leaves him few effective skills to deal with the betrayal.

When Jake came to therapy with Gracie after learning about her most recent affair, he was shocked, overwhelmed, and did not know how to cope. In the past, when matters were difficult between them, he could always count on his ability to negotiate with her or their ability to compromise. But here was a situation where neither of those responses was helpful. He was so uncomfortable admitting how angry, afraid, and disappointed he felt. With the help of the ESA exercise, Jake was eventually able to become more comfortable acknowledging his feelings. He had lived with the mistaken belief that strong men negotiate and do not get angry and never admit to having vulnerable feelings, much less needs.

Jake was able to let Gracie know how much he felt abandoned, duped, and deceived by her. In time he was also willing to admit that he had noticed changes in her but had been afraid to ask about them and did not know how to have such a conversation. Ironically, as Jake continued to share his feelings with Gracie, she began to view him as stronger, more real, less perfect, and more attractive.

■ Samantha and Paul: An Infidelity of Loneliness

Unlike Gracie and Jake, both Paul and Samantha have some rudimentary awareness of their personal dissatisfactions in the relationship. Each of them is able to acknowledge that they do not agree around finances and each does not like the way the other behaves around money issues. Paul views Samantha as fiscally irresponsible while Samantha sees Paul as controlling about money.

Paul is aware of his frustrations with Samantha, and so he tries to reason with her and share with her his fear of their financial situation. He also tries to let her know that when they disagree about money he feels insecure. Paul has the ability to acknowledge his feelings and speak up with Samantha. However, as the couple gets into the same arguments about money—Paul wanting a budget and Samantha refusing to keep within budget—he eventually gives up sharing his feelings with her. When Paul makes this choice, he has begun to limit his ability to be self-intimate. By not sharing his feelings with Samantha, he stops paying attention to other feelings; he begins to shut down his awareness of feelings of frustration, resentment, and resignation. As these feelings go unacknowledged and unexpressed, they eventually show up in arguments in which he accuses Samantha of not caring about what is important to him. While there is some truth to this feeling, many other feelings—such as hurt, feeling unimportant, undervalued, unloved, resentful, and lonely—are not acknowledged. As the couple now argues about Paul's belief that Samantha does not care about him, Paul is unaware of the other feelings he has, and, therefore, cannot do anything to express or remedy these.

His unacknowledged and unexpressed feelings lay the foundation for Paul to feel more and more separate from Samantha. Having an infidelity is the last thing on his mind. He believes he is coping with an unresolved financial issue in the best way he knows how. At this point, unfortunately, Paul is correct.

Samantha recognizes that she feels hounded by Paul about money. She has heard him say that her spending scares him, but she believes that he is exaggerating in an attempt to control her. She shares these feelings with him, but she's afraid to also let him know that she is beginning to resent him. She is uncomfortable with this strong feeling, so instead of talking about it, she tries to deny the feeling. It becomes evident when her anger inspires her to mock his feelings of fear, concern, or anger.

Samantha has some emotional self-awareness, but when faced with her own strong, negative feelings, she withdraws. Consequently, the couple is able to discuss feelings about non-combative topics, but over time the "safe" topics are fewer.

Chapter Review

Self-Intimacy is the moment-to-moment awareness of one's feelings, thoughts, and needs as well as the willingness to acknowledge and own these to oneself and with one's partner.

Why Self-Intimacy Is So Important

- The decision to be unfaithful is born here.

- SI represents the best way to take care of yourself, especially with regard to expressing negative feelings.

- SI is directly connected to your instincts.

As you look at your capacity to be self-intimate, consider how good you are at taking care of yourself by expressing your negative and positive feelings and being aware of your instincts and intuitions. There is room for improvement for any of us. Use the ESA exercise to increase your ability to be self-intimate and take care of yourself.

Emotional Self-Awareness Exercise

Ask yourself at least three times a day the following three questions:

1. What emotion(s) am I feeling right now?

2. What situation or perception of mine is causing me to feel this emotion(s)?

3. What, if anything, can I do about this causal situation to take good care of myself?

Keys to ESA: Practice makes for "perfect" Self-Intimacy

- Practice daily: five minutes, two to three times a day, for ninety days.

- Make your emotional world a priority.

chapter 6

conflict intimacy: the cornerstone of relationship resiliency

When the water starts boiling it is foolish to turn off the heat. —Nelson Mandela

It's not that I'm so smart, it's just that I stay with problems longer. —Albert Einstein

One of the great and inconvenient truths about love is that no two people are so perfectly matched that they will never hurt or disappoint each other. Even the most in love couples will sometimes be in conflict with each other.

So the question is not whether there is conflict in a Long-Term Love Relationship, but whether a couple deals with their conflicts well. You want a quick measure of an LTLR's health? Look no further than how they handle their differences. That is what separates LTLRs that are built to flourish and those that are headed for trouble.

All too often that trouble comes in the form of an infidelity, for when a partner finds himself unable to work through conflict with his partner within the bounds of their LTLR, he will often look for "resolution" to the conflict outside their relationship. It's inappropriate and it's wrong, but in combination with low Self-Intimacy, that is what leads to infidelity.

So in this chapter we are going to teach you the surest way to avoid this. We're going to show you that you can use conflict to strengthen your LTLR, to bring you and your partner closer so that infidelity never becomes a consideration. We're going to teach you how to develop Conflict Intimacy.

CONFLICT STYLES

Before we begin our exploration of Conflict Intimacy, we're going to return to the two maladaptive conflict process styles identified by Bader and Pearson (1988). You should be able to recognize you and your partner in one of the styles, or a combination, which will help you think through your personal road to Conflict Intimacy.

Hostile Dependent

A couple that is stuck in Hostile Dependent mode deals with conflict by having knock-down, drag-out fights. One or both partners use their anger to bludgeon the other, to hurt them, to get them to back down. Consequently, very little if anything ever gets resolved. Not only that, but the destructive nature of the fights adds insult to injury. The traumatic arguments make things worse, bringing more hurt feelings into the relationship, decreasing the couple's intimacy, and creating distance between them.

Conflict Avoidant

The Conflict Avoidant style is in many ways the opposite of Hostile Dependent, but it is just as destructive. Conflict Avoidant couples simply avoid conflict. They brush everything under the rug. They try to ignore problems and hope the issues and the negative feelings associated with them just go away. They don't fight, they don't deal with their differences, and they don't address their hurts, disappointments, and angers. Quite understandably, resentments build up, intimacy weakens, and they grow apart.

In some cases, a couple may fluctuate between the two conflict styles. They'll brush things under the rug for months and then have an explosion of toxic fighting. Then they'll go back to avoiding conflict for a while. The longer this pattern holds, the shorter the periods of "calm" Conflict Avoidance become. Hostile Dependent fights happen more and more frequently as the couple finds it harder and harder to ignore their pent-up pain and anger.

CONFLICT INTIMACY

The only antidote to these damaging conflict process styles is for the couple to learn how to constructively deal with their differences, to learn what we call Conflict Intimacy. Conflict Intimacy is the ability to express your negative feelings in an assertive way, without avoiding them or expressing them in an aggressive or attacking manner. It also entails learning how to really listen when your partner expresses his negative feelings, without withdrawing from him or attacking him for it. Conflict Intimacy is about holding onto yourself in the face of tension that exists between you and your partner. If a couple fails to learn these skills, their LTLR is likely to remain forever stuck in Soured Symbiosis. Conflict Intimacy enables couples to achieve the third stage of Long-Term Love Relationships, Differentiation.

The Benefits of Conflict Intimacy

Conflict in your LTLR isn't a bad thing. Think of it as growing pains, an indicator that you and your partner are struggling to move from a symbiotic level of functioning to a differentiated level, from an immature relationship to a mature one. If you can get good at dealing with your differences, you and your partner will find that this will be one of, if not the most, powerful means of enhancing the strength of your LTLR.

Conflict Intimacy allows each partner to openly and constructively voice his or her negative feelings while also being "curious, not furious" (Pete Pearson, personal communication, 2000) in the face of his or her partner's pain and anger. When a couple is conflict intimate, each person is able to remain separate in conflict—neither needs to get their partner to agree with them. They simply do a good job of standing up for themselves and hear, respect, and seek understanding of what their partner is saying. And they manage to do all this even when their partner is expressing something contrary to what they think and feel, even when it is hurtful or threatens to make their blood boil.

Sounds like a tall order, doesn't it? It is and yet it is a natural extension of the work you have already begun by pushing yourself to be self-intimate. That's the beauty of the three LTLR building blocks, the three intimacies: each one activates the next. The growth in your Self-Intimacy will lead you, in fact will push you, to be more conflict intimate. The more you are focused on taking good care of yourself based on your emotional self-awareness, the more you will share yourself openly with your partner.

The added challenge of Conflict Intimacy is holding onto yourself in the moments of emotional conflict with your partner, when you are telling him things that he won't like hearing and hearing things that you may not like at all. But rather than backing down, giving in, insisting on winning, or appeasing, when you are conflict intimate, you retain your views in a nonhostile, nondefensive way.

THE I-TO-I EXERCISE

You don't need to be a psychologist or a Zen master to become conflict intimate. You just have to develop skill in playing two roles. First, you need to learn to effectively stand up for yourself when something is bothering you in your LTLR. Second, you need to learn to nondefensively express yourself when your partner lets you know that he is upset with you. Getting good at both those roles just takes practice.

To help you develop Conflict Intimacy, we use an exercise developed by Bader and Pearson (1988), the Initiator-Inquirer or the I-to-I Exercise. It is a very effective tool in teaching couples how to develop the skills that lead to Conflict Intimacy. The I-to-I exercise consists of two roles, the Initiator and the Inquirer.

The Initiator

The Initiator's role is to bring up one issue and the emotions she has about it. The Initiator is to own this issue as her problem, and not blame or attack the partner. The Initiator's job is not to tell the partner what a heel he is, but to openly and honestly express her feelings, thoughts, and desires around the topic.

Assuming the role of the Initiator means that you are willing to really explore what is motivating your feelings on the topic. Your goal is to push yourself to understand various aspects of your feelings and how this issue is a problem for you. You are committed to understanding yourself better and to helping your partner know your reality.

The Initiator agrees to talk about herself only. She gives her perspective and is specific about her feelings. This exercise is often the most beneficial when you discuss a topic that you are afraid to share, that you are afraid will anger your partner, or are afraid will cause you embarrassment. Structure your sharing around the answers to the first two questions of the Emotional Self-Awareness Exercise, such as "I feel x because of y." Don't blame your partner. Remember, your responsibility is to talk about yourself. And, lastly, your goal is to help your partner know your reality on this topic, not to convince him that your reality is *the* reality.

The Inquirer

The Inquirer's role is to listen, recap what he heard the Initiator say, and then ask questions about what she shared. The

Inquirer agrees to listen to what the Initiator is sharing and to suspend his view of the topic during this discussion. His job is to hear the Initiator's view and respect it while not challenging it with his own view.

The Inquirer is not passive in this exercise. In many ways, the Inquirer serves as a mirror for the Initiator. After the Initiator is done talking, she may not recall all of what she said because she is experiencing some strong emotions. So, as the Inquirer recaps her words, he is also helping her to hear herself. This summary should be made without any editorial comment—the feelings, thinking, and topic should simply be stated.

After the Inquirer has summarized what the Initiator said, he asks questions designed to help him understand his partner and help her further understand herself. He should ask questions about what she has brought up, but not with reference to his own point of view. His questions should not be designed to defend himself. The Inquirer's job is to learn about his partner, to accept the intimate piece of the Initiator that is being shared, even when it is painful and especially when he sees things differently.

The Inquirer needs to fight getting defensive. Throughout the exercise, the Inquirer needs to remind himself that what his partner is sharing is about her, not him, no matter how many times she references him. That is why we often tell clients in the Inquirer role that their mantra needs to be "It's not about me; it's not about me; it's not about me."

And, lastly, the Inquirer needs to resist the temptation to problem solve. He needs to maintain his commitment to respond to the discussion differently than he has in the past.

Practicing Without Your Partner's Active Participation

While learning Conflict Intimacy and practicing the I-to-I are quicker and more effective when you and your partner are working on them together, you can still learn the skills on your own. When you're in conversation with your partner, your job will be to recognize when you are the Initiator and when you are the Inquirer.

Practicing the Inquirer

For example, your partner begins to argue with you about the fact that he's just returned from work and you've been home for a couple of hours and the kitchen is a mess. In this case he is the Initiator. Rather than defending yourself, attacking him, or avoiding the discussion, you assume the role of the Inquirer and tell him what you heard him say. It might sound something like this:

You (Inquirer):	You're frustrated and angry that you've had a long day and you've walked in the house and the kitchen is a mess. Having a messy kitchen at this point in your day is really difficult for you.
Partner (Initiator, unbeknownst to him):	Yeah, it's the last thing I need! If you cared at all about me and what's important to me, you'd clean it!
You (Inquirer):	It's really important to you that I show that I care about you and how you're feeling. I'll be glad to clean it up.

Note that you stood at a crossroads when your partner came back at you. Because of his attitude, tone, and unkind way of asking, many of us might refuse to do what he's demanding. Or we might resentfully comply because we're so uncomfortable with the situation and don't want it to get any worse. But remember that you are reading this book because he had an infidelity and you want some new options for dealing with conflict.

Hearing what your partner has to say in spite of his harsh or unreasonable delivery is certainly a new approach. Your goal would be to give him what he is requesting without resenting it, even while you may still dislike his tone. Often when the conversation goes this way, the angry, demanding partner eases up and is able to see how harsh he has been. It's difficult to remain hostile when the other person doesn't respond in kind.

It's often helpful to practice the I-to-I in conversations with other people too. For example, you're at lunch with a girlfriend and she begins to share about her marital difficulties. You recognize that she is the Initiator so you assume the role of Inquirer and tell her what you heard her say; reflect back to her to see if you understood her correctly. You'll likely find she is relieved to know you're listening and that she is making sense. Again, rather than having a less structured conversation, you can ask her questions about what she has said, stay where she is on the topic, and continue to explore her perspective. Refrain from offering your opinion or adding how you have experienced something similar. Try this for about ten minutes.

At first, you will find this interchange somewhat awkward. But, with continued practice, we guarantee that you will find yourself understanding your friend more deeply, though you may not agree with her. In order to help you solidify the changed way of communicating, after the ten-minute trial, ask her if you can offer your insights. By doing this, you are asking if she is ready to stop sharing and if she is open to an alternative view. If she says yes, then she is more likely to be willing to hear and consider what you have to say.

Practicing the Initiator

For example, you've made tentative dinner plans with another couple and you then tell your partner about it. He responds with anger because you didn't check with him first. In the past you would have defended yourself, argued with him, or criticized him for being angry. This time you recognize that you want to talk about your feelings and handle the situation better by assuming the Initiator role. You start by talking with your husband about what you did, what you want, and how you feel. It might sound something like this:

You (Initiator):   John, when Sally called today and invited us out to dinner with her and Bob it sounded interesting and fun. So I told her yes, but that I would have to check with you.

Partner:	The restaurant sounds good, but do I really have a choice since you already told her yes?
You (Initiator):	You do have a choice. But, before we get to that, I want you to know that it's important to me to be able to tentatively respond to people in situations like this and that you will discuss the choice with me rather than immediately responding with anger. (You are not reacting; you continue to talk about yourself.)
Partner:	But if I say no, then I look like the bad guy.
You (Initiator):	No one is the bad guy. This isn't about you. This is about me realizing that I'm often afraid to bring these kinds of things up with you because you might get angry. I don't want to be treated like that anymore. (You continue to hold onto yourself and share your feelings and motivations.)
Partner:	Well, the restaurant sounds good. It's just that I don't like to look bad or feel like my weekend is scheduled for me.
You (Initiator):	I understand your needs, but I'm not sure you're hearing mine. I need to be able to make choices and know that you will be receptive and not jump to anger. I want to know that you give me the benefit of the doubt and know that my intentions are good. You don't have to agree with me, but I do want you to discuss things with me. I want to talk like two equals instead of just getting anger from you.

Partner:	That's reasonable. I do jump to conclusions. Sorry I jumped down your throat.
You (Initiator):	Thanks, I really appreciate that. So does Saturday work for you?

Notice that while your partner may be continuing to assume a somewhat defensive or hostile response, you continue to talk about yourself: your feelings, thoughts, and desires. Many of us might try to convince or talk the other person into our viewpoint or out of theirs. Once we try to do this, we stop talking about our feelings and thoughts and begin to defend ourselves. As we know, this choice is not helpful to the conversation or the relationship.

Staying with what you have to say in a non-defensive way is a different approach. Your goal is to talk about yourself and your intentions. Often when the conversation goes this way, the defensive or angry partner is able to hear your intentions more clearly. Even if he doesn't, you have nothing to lose as you are representing yourself more accurately and that feels better for you.

Each time you practice the role of the Initiator you will become more comfortable sharing your experience, and you will find it becomes easier not to return to your old way of getting stuck in the conversation. With time, your conversations can become more productive and less competitive and/or argumentative.

Practicing with Your Partner's Active Participation

You may have heard that one definition of insanity is doing the same thing over and over and expecting a different result. If you want change, you need to be an agent of change. Just doing one thing different can be the beginning of change. You've been reading this book and practicing changes. If you are going to have any chance of healing your LTLR and making it infidelity invulnerable, now is the time to invite your partner to join you in making those changes. If he refuses, your LTLR has little hope of healing, let alone thriving.

As you introduce this book and what you're learning to your partner, it is important you do so from a clear, honest position, not one of weakness (by pleading) or demanding (by being self-righteous). Talk with your partner about what you have discovered about yourself and how you have been working on changing. Ask him if he's noticed any changes in you. If he says no, that does not necessarily mean that your efforts are in vain. Change takes time, patience, and many opportunities.

But obviously, you're not the primary person who needs to make changes here: he was the one who was unfaithful. He needs to take a lot of responsibility for leading change in the relationship. And he needs to work on himself. Remember, unless he clearly accepts these responsibilities, there is little chance that you can be happy or safe with him in the future.

Ask your partner to read this book and to let you know when he has gotten to this chapter. At this point, you can discuss beginning to try the I-to-I together. It is important that your first practice session be at an agreed time and that you recognize that the exercise will initially be awkward for both of you. It might be helpful to make copies of the I-to-I guidelines (see appendix B) for each of you to review before your discussion.

The I-to-I Format

To start the exercise off, each of you should specifically state what you would like to work on. Then you should agree upon one topic to discuss. Next you need to decide who will be the Initiator and who will be the Inquirer.

We recommend that your first I-to-I exercises focus on what is currently going on in your relationship or new insights that you might have had since reading this book. While the roles are clearly defined, you are likely to find that as the feelings expressed get more intense, the Inquirer may have more and more difficulty recapping. The Initiator should help by calmly repeating what she said, without any criticism of the Inquirer's struggle. Usually couples find that they can only get through fifteen to twenty minutes of the I-to-I the first few times.

Sometimes couples ask us if they can take notes when listening to their partner. We discourage this, as it can be distracting. You should be considering your partner a friend with whom you can discuss anything, and try to just listen without any investment in the outcome. It's important to remember that you do not have to change no matter what your partner says. This will assist you in listening and hearing your partner.

Also, the Initiator and the Inquirer should not be keeping score of the other's progress. Each person's focus needs to remain on their role in the exercise. Both roles present challenges. As the Initiator, you are likely to struggle to talk about yourself and keep the focus on your feelings versus your demands or your anger and blame. The Inquirer may struggle to not react defensively to what the Initiator is saying, and to not correct or interject.

The first time you try this exercise, stop after you find yourselves getting bogged down. Then each of you should take a turn talking about how it was to be in the role you assumed. You are not to evaluate how the other person did. Only comment on your own experience in the role.

We recommend that you and your partner use this format at least twice a week for twenty minutes each time the first week, then increase the time by ten minutes each succeeding week. By the fourth week, you should be ready to use the format whenever you and your partner discuss an issue.

Conflict Intimacy Progress

Bader and Krohn (1996) have diagrammed what Initiators and Inquirers do as they progress from being emotionally immature to mature in their roles. This progression is illustrated in the I-to-I Maturity Goals Handout (see appendix C). After you first practice the I-to-I, take a look at the descriptions of what motivates each person in the Initiator or Inquirer role. You can clearly see how number 1 represents the least mature response, while the higher numbers represent the most mature.

For example, the Initiator goals are outlined from the sentence stem, "When something is bothering me . . ." The most immature response, number 1, states that "I recognize when I am upset, but I don't bring up my feelings."

Contrast this with number 5, which marks the beginning of emotional maturity: "I stop and think about what is bothering me and why, before I talk to my partner about it." This difference is noteworthy: in number 5, the Initiator is able to identify what her concern is and how it evolved, and then initiate a discussion.

Then look at number 7, further along the maturity progression: "I tell my partner what the problem is and what my feelings are without blaming." And, lastly, the most mature way to be an Initiator is indicated by number 10: "Throughout the conversation I am interested in learning and discovering more about myself and how I function."

After you and your partner have practiced the I-to-I once, try again. Decide on the topic and the role each of you will assume and then look over the Maturity Goals Handout. Each of you should choose a goal for that conversation. That is, if you are the Initiator, you look over the goals handout and decide, for example, that you want to work on number 7: "I tell my partner what the problem is and what my feelings are without blaming him." Then you keep this goal in mind as you talk about your concern in the I-to-I format.

In turn, your partner will look at the handout for the Inquirer and determine his goal. It might be number 7: "I ask questions designed to deepen my understanding of my partner." Your partner has likely chosen this goal because he has recognized that he often gets off track in the exercise by trying to find a solution or wanting to bring up his viewpoint. During the exercise, he then keeps his goal in mind to help himself stay on track.

The more you and your partner use the role goals, the more effective you'll both be as Initiators and Inquirers. As Initiators, you'll be better able to talk about yourself and learn about your concerns. As Inquirers, you'll be better listeners who assist your partner in learning more about themselves. You'll make progress (individually and as a couple) at times and get stuck (individually and as a couple) at other times. There are different challenges for each of you in either role.

With some topics, you may find that you are more easily able to function maturely in one role than in the other. You will also find that you can get to a certain point and then start regressing as the discussion becomes more emotionally difficult. For example, as the Inquirer, you may find yourself unable to summarize what your partner has said or find it difficult to be curious as the conversation gets more intense. Or, as Initiator, you may find that you stop discussing your feelings, or begin to blame or want a solution from your partner.

This tendency to get stuck is normal and indicates that you have arrived at your current Conflict Intimacy limit. However, we encourage you to continue on with the exercise for five more minutes (as the Initiator) or ask two more questions (as the Inquirer). This will help you make some progress and grow beyond your limits. Progress is the goal, not perfection.

Key Points

When practicing the I-to-I exercise, there are a couple key points to remember that will make your work a lot easier and help you make sense of what you're going through.

It's Just an Exercise

After practicing the I-to-I for a while, some couples will ask, "Is this how we're supposed to talk all the time?" The answer is no. It's just an exercise, and a very restrictive one at that. It's not meant to be used in all your interactions with your partner. That would be way too tedious.

This is simply a way to teach you some skills, to give you tools to hold in reserve for when necessary. What we're doing is teaching you how to stand up for yourself in a strong, constructive, nonattacking way, and how to react nondefensively when your partner gets upset with you. The exercise shows you how to really hear and understand your partner's reality, even when it is diametrically opposed to your own.

So don't worry; you don't have to talk with him like this all the time. But with dedicated practice of the I-to-I, the two of you will become proficient at using these tools so that conflict will no longer divide you. Instead, working through your conflicts will bring you closer.

Process, Not Resolution

To the great frustration of many couples, the I-to-I exercise does not help them resolve their conflicts at all. While finding healthy resolutions is important, mistakes in how they go through the conflict process is often what stymies couples, which in turn keeps them from getting to a healthy resolution.

We often find that when a couple is first learning the I-to-I exercise, we have to stop them from reflexively moving into problem-solving mode. To reduce the tension they're feeling and to counteract the fear of continuing their old patterns, they often prematurely try to find resolution. At this point, we try to get them to stop and focus on how to handle the tension itself. In addition, settling a conflict through premature resolution rarely serves to actually resolve anything.

The only way to increase tension tolerance is to systematically work through the process of unresolved conflict. This is how you will discover more about each other and will eventually be able to arrive at solutions you could not have anticipated before.

RECOGNIZING AND BREAKING OUT OF YOUR OLD CONFLICT STYLE

As you and your partner practice the I-to-I exercise, keep in mind what your old, toxic conflict style was. Were you a Conflict Avoidant couple or a Hostile Dependent one? Remembering which style got you into this mess will help you work to break out of it.

If your old style was Conflict Avoidant, then you'll really have to work to manage your anxiety and not let it control you. Disagreement makes people who are Conflict Avoidant very nervous; that's why they'll do just about anything to not be in conflict. This anxiety often manifests in the I-to-I through a push toward premature resolution. Be aware of your anxiety. Examine it. What do you really have to be afraid of? The reality is that you have much more to fear if you don't stay in the conversation. Push yourself to keep talking; if you don't, you will never acquire good Conflict Intimacy skills with your partner.

If your old style was Hostile Dependent, then you're going to have to work hard not to let your anger control you. As the Initiator, you'll need to focus on not attacking and blaming. As the Inquirer, think about not getting defensive, not attacking back, not falling into using offense as the best defense.

Anger itself isn't bad, but you aren't serving yourself or your partner by wielding it in a destructive way. Folks who are Hostile Dependent use their anger as a way to defend themselves. But in defending yourself from your partner, you are actually pushing him away. At some point, you're going to have to let go of your anger or the two of you can never become close.

Bader and Pearson's I-to-I exercise is a powerful tool because it focuses on conflict process rather than conflict resolution; it gives couples tools with which to work through conflict. As you and your partner practice the I-to-I and learn to discuss topics even while disagreeing, you develop Conflict Intimacy and escape your old intimacy-killing conflict pattern, whether it is Conflict Avoidant or Hostile Dependent.

THE MOST POWERFUL RELATIONSHIP ENHANCER

When individuals and couples have done good work on developing Self-Intimacy and Conflict Intimacy, the third intimacy, Affection Intimacy, improves and deepens. Self-Intimacy enables Conflict Intimacy, and Conflict Intimacy is the foundation upon which Affection Intimacy can then be built.

But we consider Conflict Intimacy to be the true initiator of relationship change, growth, resilience, and hope; it is the most powerful relationship enhancer. As you and your partner begin to have successful conflict experiences, you, like the couples we have worked with, will begin to feel closer to each other. You will again see your partner as the person you fell in love with instead of someone you view with anger and disappointment.

As this change happens, you will both begin to have hope and renewed confidence in each other and in your relationship. This greater sense of safety and security helps you both see that you are truly partners on this journey.

By becoming conflict intimate, you and your partner ensure that you'll be able to successfully navigate the natural but some-times difficult terrain that comes with every relationship. In the face of conflict and tension, you and your partner will be able to get through your differences. This will make your LTLR bond stronger. It will serve as a powerful means of precluding the future possibility of an infidelity, guaranteed.

CONFLICT INTIMACY IN PRACTICE

Now let's take a peek into the relationships of two of our companion couples to learn just how Conflict Intimacy plays such a crucial role in LTLRs.

■ Amy and Lewis: An Infidelity of Anger

Amy and Lewis are a Hostile Dependent couple; they deal with their disappointments and differences by remaining stuck in their arguments, convinced that they will eventually persuade or wear down their partner into agreeing with them.

Lewis has not been able to tolerate the disappointment that he feels in the marriage and has begun to believe that he deserves consolation from someone. "After all," he reasons, "if Amy won't meet my needs, then I deserve to get them met elsewhere!"

Amy finds Lewis's expressions of anger unjustified. She believes he is "just an angry man who only knows how to express frustrations and negative experiences as anger." She alternates between avoiding his anger, lashing back at him, trying to out-argue or out-guilt him, and withdrawing in fear and resignation. In all of these reactions, she lacks the ability to resolve the conflict effectively.

Lewis and Amy are very limited in their Conflict Intimacy. Amy is desperate for Lewis's approval and is afraid of his disapproval. Lewis is afraid that Amy will leave him, and he's angry with himself and with her that he needs her so badly. Unfortunately, neither is able to constructively work on these feelings with the other.

Both Amy and Lewis are dissatisfied with the marriage and agree that the most passion they have is when they are angry and fighting. Sex isn't that frequent or satisfying. They are both stuck in their blame and anger and are unwilling to extend an olive branch. At this juncture, their relationship is in real trouble. Soon Amy will discover credit card receipts, telephone numbers, and e-mails that indicate that Lewis has been with other women.

The discovery of Lewis's infidelity opens the floodgates for Amy. If she has ever felt vindicated it is now; however, by her berating Lewis, the couple just continues what they have always done but with a greater level of damage to each other and to the relationship.

Amy could not tolerate the hurt of the betrayal and the continuing cycle of arguing. She called for a therapy appointment. Lewis reluctantly agreed to come with her, but was not comfortable having her come to an appointment and risk that she'd misrepresent the issues.

Amy and Lewis were accustomed to telling their story by competing over whose version was more accurate. Despite their anger, it was clear how much each of them was hurting and felt the need to protect themselves. In spite of their desire to continue arguing for both the safety and familiarity it provided them, they each reluctantly agreed to learn a new way to talk about their conflicts.

Each was asked what they wanted to work on and both offered topics: Amy wanted to discuss the hurt and anger she had about the betrayal, and Lewis wanted to talk about how he felt driven to be unfaithful.

The I-to-I exercise was introduced to them and then they were asked which of the topics they would agree to discuss. After much jockeying, Lewis agreed to listen to Amy discuss her hurt. As the Initiator, Amy was reminded that her goal was not to blame Lewis but to describe and explore her feelings and really let Lewis and herself know how she felt about the betrayal.

Lewis as the Inquirer agreed to suspend his view of the betrayal and listen to Amy's experience. He would try to hear what she felt, recap her feelings, and then ask questions related to what she shared.

Amy struggled to avoid blaming Lewis. She also found herself fearful of discovering the feelings beneath her anger such as fear and disappointment. With repeated work as the Initiator, she was able to learn that she feared being abandoned by Lewis and had a deep belief that she was not worthy of love.

Amy had to struggle not to get stuck in mostly blaming Lewis rather than discovering her feelings and being willing to stay honest with Lewis no matter what response he might make. She also learned (through much practice) that she could tolerate being vulnerable with Lewis and that her sense of self and personal strength came from her ability to share her feelings rather than from his acceptance or agreement with her feelings. Amy realized how much she used to fight with Lewis in an attempt to get him to agree with her so she could feel good about herself.

As an Initiator, she learned to value her own feelings and to hold onto them in the face of disagreement—not for the sake of argument, to get agreement, or to change her partner's mind, but for the purposes of holding onto herself.

Once Amy was able to state her feelings, she felt less need to argue or convince Lewis. She found herself able to share her hurt, devastation, and her need to feel cherished and protected in a relationship. The more she discovered and shared her feelings, the less desperate she eventually felt. She admitted that she wanted to save her marriage, but was willing to face the possibility that Lewis might not be capable of being the kind of partner she wanted and felt she deserved. She was able to say this to Lewis without blaming or threatening him, but in the spirit of sharing herself.

As Amy shared her feelings as the Initiator, Lewis struggled to suspend his views and listen to her feelings in his role as the Inquirer. With assistance he was able to tell her what he heard her say. This was very difficult for Lewis. He needed to be reminded that while he heard and respected Amy's experience he was not expected to change his view. With practice, Lewis was able to hear Amy's feelings and not take them personally. He fought the impulse to blame her and minimize her feelings. As he made progress hearing her experience, he began to hear how his actions had affected her.

Lewis was eventually able to acknowledge that while he had intended to hurt Amy by having affairs, he did not realize the extent of pain that the betrayal would cause her.

As Lewis was able to hear his wife's feelings as being about her and not an attempt to attack or criticize him, he started to feel less defensive. He then could begin to distinguish between the pain he directly caused and the fears and hurts she had that had not been caused by him.

Amy's practice as an Initiator helped her to define and express her feelings to Lewis and created in her a separate self. At the same time, Lewis's ability to hear his wife's experience as her own freed him up to stop trying to talk her in or out of a feeling and allowed him to respect her separate experiences without feeling he was losing or giving up a part of himself.

These changes laid the foundation for Amy and Lewis to begin to break out of their destructive Hostile Dependent pattern and showed them a safe way to express themselves as separate people who did not need the other person to agree or accede to their view in order to feel accepted in the relationship.

■ Cindy and Scott: Growing Pains Without Infidelity

Cindy's ability to be self-intimate is pretty good, while Scott's is a bit more limited. Cindy is often aware of both her positive and negative feelings and shares them with Scott. However as the couple entered Soured Symbiosis and Scott reacted with anger and defensiveness when she expressed her anger and/or frustration, Cindy began to share less and less openly with Scott. Consequently, she began to have greater feelings of disappointment and anger toward Scott.

Unfortunately, Scott is both unfamiliar and uncomfortable with negative feelings, so when Cindy expresses negative feelings he finds himself feeling attacked and becomes disappointed with the relationship. He has entered Soured Symbiosis, and the only way he knows to try to get back to Sweet Symbiosis is to avoid negative feelings. He believes that people should compromise and that anger and negative feelings are bad or at least unnecessary. In the face of disagreement, he withdraws and becomes Conflict Avoidant, or he attempts to up the ante by intimidating Cindy with his anger. This choice leads him to avoid his own negative feelings and limits his Self-Intimacy. Now strapped with Soured Symbiosis and avoidance as his tool to deal with negativity, he feels cornered and attacked when Cindy brings up what is bothering her.

At this point both Cindy and Scott have limited their ability to be more self-intimate, which, in turn, makes it difficult for them to talk through their differences or be conflict intimate. When conflict arises, Cindy overreacts rather than talking about her feelings and needs while Scott accuses and defends himself. After one especially bitter argument, Scott gave us a call requesting marriage counseling.

They were each asked what they wanted to work on. Cindy offered the topic of Scott's anger and how he cuts off difficult discussions by withdrawing or attacking. Scott suggested discussing how Cindy never seemed satisfied with him. The I-to-I format was presented and the couple agreed to talk about Scott's anger. Scott agreed to be the Initiator and to focus on his many feelings while Cindy was the Inquirer who would suspend her view and listen to Scott's experience and feelings.

Scott initially wanted to blame Cindy and described what she commonly did to provoke him. With redirection, he was slowly able to talk about how he felt attacked, criticized, anxious, and "less than" when Cindy expressed negative feelings about him. Cindy struggled in her role as Inquirer to hear Scott's experience and to respect it. She wanted to interrupt him, correct him, and offer her defense. She was responsive to suggestions to breathe, calm herself, and tell Scott what she heard him say without editorial comment.

The I-to-I exercise was slow and steady going for them. Over time Scott was able to define his feelings and realize how often he reacted to Cindy's negative feelings as if he was being blamed or accused. As he switched roles and practiced being the Inquirer, he came to hear that Cindy was attempting to talk about their differences because she wanted their relationship to be better. Her aim wasn't to win, be right, or "nail" him (goals 8 and 9, Inquirer role, Maturity Goals Handout). Scott also became more adept at recognizing his own feelings (Self-Intimacy) and being able to talk about his negative feelings in a way that was not explosive or cumulative (goals 5 and 6, *Initiator role*, Maturity Goals Handout).

For her part, Cindy began to realize how much she overreacted to a man's anger. She saw how her anxiety and fear had caused her to respond by trying to talk Scott out of his anger. She gradually was able to hear and respect his anger and not necessarily conclude that all of it was "her fault." She eventually realized that she could have a part in his anger but wasn't the total cause of it. For example, she recognized that when she broadsided him with her feelings of hurt or anger he was more likely to get angry. So, she changed her behavior and would ask Scott for a good time to talk (goal 6, Initiator role, Maturity Goals Handout) and found that then they were both prepared to talk.

From the Initiator role, Cindy also learned the price she and the relationship had been paying for her silence when she had given up on sharing feelings with Scott. She recognized that not only had she been withholding negative feelings, but that positive ones had also been sacrificed. She pushed herself to express her angry and disappointed feelings to Scott even though he might react harshly. Then she was eventually able to soothe herself and matter-of-factly tell him that she was feeling anxious and that she wanted to continue to talk with him, asking him if he could let her continue (goal 8, Initiator role, Maturity Goals Handout).

What These Two Couples Teach You

Both couples' inability to successfully navigate conflict made them grow apart and begin to feel less intimate and less satisfied with their relationship. Because Lewis allowed his anger to both control his view of Amy and motivate his actions, he sought affairs. Amy was stuck in her unsuccessful retaliatory anger. Cindy tried to discuss conflict but eventually gave up and resentfully withdrew, while Scott vacillated between avoiding all anger or eventually using it to intimidate his wife.

Both couples want a close, strong relationship, but they didn't know how to get past their differences and conflicts. Their limited Conflict Intimacy skills had led them to the rocky road of relationship stresses, conflict, and disappointment. The anger and conflict caused Lewis to lose enough faith in the strength and capacity of their relationship, eventually leading him to choose infidelities. With Conflict Intimacy skills and the Maturity Goals in hand, both these couples now have the best chance to both heal and rebuild their relationship to be an LTLR.

Chapter Review

The Importance of Conflict Intimacy

Conflict Intimacy is the ability to acknowledge and express your feelings with yourself and your partner, to hear the same from your partner, and remain in the conversation process until the two of you arrive at a mutually agreed upon resolution.

- The acid test of an LTLR is not how bad the stresses are that the couple is dealing with, but how well they deal with those stresses. The key ability for any couple to develop is Conflict

Intimacy, the ability to effectively handle stress
and the conflicts that stress causes.

■   Conflict Intimacy tool: The Initiator-Inquirer or
the I-to-I exercise

How able are you to hang in there and listen to your partner's negative feelings about you? How good are you at expressing
your negative feelings about him without blaming or criticizing
him? Most of us have room for improvement. Practice both the
Initiator and Inquirer roles to increase your ability to be both a
good listener and a capable Initiator.

The I-to-I Exercise

■   *The Initiator:* The person who agrees to share with
his/her partner difficult feelings about an issue and
is committed to learning more about his/her
feelings, thoughts, and needs while trying not to
blame his/her partner.

■   *The Inquirer:* This partner agrees to suspend
his/her view of the problem or issue being
discussed while actively listening to the Initiator's
feelings, thoughts, and needs around the issue.
The Inquirer recaps for the Initiator what he/she
heard without any editorial comment and asks
questions to further understand the Initiator's
feelings.

■   *How to practice:* We suggest an initial practice of
fifteen minutes to be increased by five-minute
intervals with each practice.

■   *The I-to-I Maturity Goals:* After the first two
experiences with the I-to-I, use the Maturity Goals
Handout to set a goal for yourself in the role of
Initiator or Inquirer.

Reminders

- It's just an exercise.

- Focus on the process, not resolution.

- One of your goals is to increase your tolerance for tension and differences in the relationship.

- Another goal is to make the focus of a conversation understanding and respect for yourself and your partner rather than agreement.

- Push yourself to avoid the lure to return to your old style of reacting.

- And finally, another objective is to learn and choose to respond rather than simply react.

chapter 7

affection intimacy: the foundation of your relationship

Marriage is a door which looks out upon a beautiful view. As that door is opened and the horizon unfolds before you, know that nothing is sweeter than the warmth of one hand within another.
—Collin McCarty

We all crave affection. Receiving affection from our beloved and giving it back to him or her is one of the most beautiful and magical experiences we can have.

That's how your relationship started out, isn't it? It was full of loving, so wonderful.

But somewhere along the way that changed. That strong bond you had diminished. Sweet Symbiosis ended, as it always does. You two have probably been struggling to get it back ever since.

You can get it back, though it's never quite the same as it was in the beginning. This time around it will be deeper and richer. That's why we've been teaching you about Self-Intimacy (SI) and Conflict Intimacy (CI), the first two building blocks that enable you to build your relationship on solid ground. Affection Intimacy is the next step, a way to strengthen your connection through expressions of warmth, love, and passion.

In this chapter, we'll explain exactly what Affection Intimacy (AI) is, what its role in your LTLR needs to be, and how it's related to and dependent upon Self-Intimacy and Conflict Intimacy.

AFFECTION INTIMACY DEFINED

Affection Intimacy is what makes Sweet Symbiosis sweet. It is everything that you and your partner do that expresses love for each other, from sweet things to thoughtful things to passionate things. Love powers your acts of Affection Intimacy and, in turn, is strengthened and deepened by acts of mutual affection between you and your partner.

Affection Intimacy changes in the course of a relationship. When a relationship first develops, it is full of passionate, intense emotion and desire. Some of that intenseness may wane over time, hopefully replaced by deeper, richer love and affection.

But that early intensity of feeling is central in providing the glue for your relationship. It cements the strong bond between you and your partner. That bond, sealed with Affection Intimacy, is what later motivates both of you to work on the relationship and have faith that it can grow and improve.

The Four Types of Affection Intimacy

Affection in LTLRs takes many forms, but we have found that they can be summed up by four types: Verbal Affection Intimacy, Actions Affection Intimacy, Sexual Affection Intimacy, and Nonsexual Physical Affection Intimacy.

Verbal Affection Intimacy

This is the verbal expression of love for your partner in all its forms, from telling him you love him to writing him a love letter to whispering sweet nothings in his ear. All the things that you say to express your love for him fit in the category of Verbal Affection Intimacy.

Actions Affection Intimacy

This category comprises all the actions that you and your partner do to express love for each other. Everything you do to take care of each other, everything you do just because you know he will like it, and everything you do to make his life easier goes in this category. Every time you do something because you love him and want to make him happy, even though you're not wild about the idea—that is Actions Affection Intimacy.

Sexual Affection Intimacy

Sexual Affection Intimacy is defined by all the sexual inter-actions between you and your partner. Intimate and passionate interplay between the two of you is essential for your LTLR to be healthy and fulfilling over the long term. Sexual touch, making out, oral sex, sexual massage, and all forms of making love are included here.

Nonsexual Physical Affection Intimacy

Nonsexual physical affection can be just as important as sexual touch to an LTLR. Any kind of touch is a very powerful expression of affection for us humans. We respond to it and yearn for it, either knowingly or unknowingly, when it is absent. Simple physical contact, like holding hands, hugging, stroking each other's back or cheek, or a quick kiss, can mean a lot in the day-to-day life of an LTLR.

FEAST OR FAMINE

Affection Intimacy is the food that sustains your Long-Term Love Relationship. Without it, your love will starve. Our partner should be our primary source for fulfilling our need for affection.

Just like with food, AI can be delicious or it can be bland. AI becomes bland when it is offered in a perfunctory way, without any feeling, when it is given more out of obligation than out of desire and caring.

Conversely, when acts of Affection Intimacy are infused with caring for your partner, they deliciously sustain your LTLR. The best, happiest relationships are those in which the two partners give each other this kind of loving affection on a daily basis. Those are well-fed LTLRs, relationships that both partners feel lucky to be in.

Different Affection Intimacy Profiles

That doesn't mean that Affection Intimacy looks the same in all strong LTLRs. For many people, some kinds of AI come naturally and other kinds don't. For example, many men in our culture are not very good at Verbal Affection Intimacy and are somewhat uncomfortable with Nonsexual Physical Affection Intimacy. But those same men may be very good at expressing their love through Actions Affection Intimacy and Sexual Affection Intimacy.

The important thing here is to be conscious of what your relationship's Affection Intimacy profile is. How good are you at the four types of AI? How about your partner? All four types are important for the health of your LTLR, so you want to appreciate and reinforce where each of you is strong and work on improving your areas of weakness.

AFFECTION INTIMACY IS BUILT ON CONFLICT INTIMACY

Unfortunately, really improving Affection Intimacy in your relationship isn't a simple matter. Without first attending to the first two building blocks of your LTLR, Self-Intimacy and Conflict Intimacy, whatever efforts you make to strengthen the Affection Intimacy in your relationship will not be successful.

Affection Intimacy does not exist in a vacuum. You can't force yourself to feel warm and loving and close with your partner if you're really feeling distant and upset. Just as you can't have strong Conflict Intimacy without good Self-Intimacy, you and your partner can't have beautiful, long-term Affection Intimacy without good Conflict Intimacy.

Passion, Dark and Light

A common misconception in Western culture is that passion is only positive, that it consists solely of the wonderful, warm, hot, loving, close aspect of intimate relating. What is overlooked is that passion has another side, a dark side. Passion is also felt in the negative feelings between two people in an LTLR. Interestingly, the English word "passion" is derived from the Latin word *passion*, which means "suffering" (*Random House Dictionary* 1987).

The dark side of passion emerges when a couple is having a heated conflict over something. It can be just as "hot" as the amorous, positive side because the emotions involved, like hurt, disappointment, anger, or rage, can be just as powerful.

Good Fighting Leads to Good Loving

In order for a couple to be truly happy in their LTLR, they have to do both sides of passion well. More specifically, unless a couple is good at handling the dark side, the light side of their passion will weaken and wither away over time.

Those couples with the strongest Affection Intimacy also have the strongest Conflict Intimacy. When a couple is still in the Sweet Symbiosis stage of their love relationship, their AI is self-sustaining and conflict is all but nonexistent. But once that honeymoon phase is over, conflict emerges and the passionate love and affection they shared is threatened. Instead of being self-sustaining, their AI now becomes dependent on their ability to effectively deal with their conflicts and the dark side of their passion.

Think about what happened in your relationship as you exited Sweet Symbiosis and the differences between the two of you started to surface; your Affection Intimacy was challenged by the emerging tensions. At this crossroads, your Affection Intimacy changed. Maybe your sexuality cooled, perhaps your verbal expressions of affection were less frequent, and you and your partner did fewer kind things for each other. This is normal and does not necessarily signal that the relationship was doomed or in trouble, but if you and your partner ignored these changes, problems and the distance between you undoubtedly grew, ending so painfully in infidelity.

Affection Intimacy cannot last if a couple deals with their differences by avoiding conflict. Neither can it be sustained if they engage in conflict in destructive, toxic ways, hurting each other more and resolving little or none of their differences.

Conversely, if a couple engages in conflict using the tools of Conflict Intimacy, their Affection Intimacy will deepen, flourish, and support their growing LTLR. Couples who process conflict well resolve their differences and through that strengthen the bond between them. From that closeness springs Affection Intimacy, acts of loving kindness.

GETTING AFFECTION INTIMACY BACK AFTER AN INFIDELITY

One of the worst casualties of infidelity is Affection Intimacy. After you found out that your partner had betrayed you, probably the last thing you felt like doing was expressing your affection for him.

Sometimes betrayed partners stay stuck in that angry, non-trusting, distant, even punishing place. Sometimes they'll soon swing to the other extreme, being solicitous, highly affectionate, and even hypersexual, in an attempt to win their partner back.

Neither of those options is productive for the long term. Neither one will enable you to reclaim your lost Affection Intimacy and rebuild your LTLR.

We will address this in more detail in chapter 12, but rest assured Affection Intimacy can be found again. You can get your love back. The secret is to understand that an infidelity, while one of the most painful things anyone can go through, can be overcome just like any other conflict or trauma. It takes time, it takes you and your partner's commitment, and it takes Self-Intimacy and Conflict Intimacy. If you have those things, your love will come back, stronger than before. If you have those things, the Affection Intimacy in your relationship will again flourish.

AFFECTION INTIMACY IN PRACTICE

The way other couples have incorporated Affection Intimacy into their LTLR can help you shine a light on the role AI has played in your relationship. Check out some of the moves your companion couples made in their AI dance.

■ Gracie and Jake: An Infidelity of Fear

Their relationship began with much mutual sexual interest, many acts of consideration, and some encouraging and loving words; however, after settling into the groove of marriage, planning a future with children, and maintaining extended family relations, Gracie found herself feeling less excited and amorous toward Jake. She acknowledged to herself that she loved, respected, and admired him, but the passion and excitement seemed to be missing for her. She attributed the change to the distractions of their lives and responded positively to Jake's sexual initiations and continued to be considerate and thankful in both her words and actions. She hoped Jake would not notice the difference in her. And, once she began having her affairs, she was especially diligent to act in loving and affectionate ways toward Jake so that he wouldn't suspect anything.

Throughout the marriage Jake reported that he had always felt excited and affectionate about Gracie. In fact, the more their lives grew with children and a home, the more he felt satisfied. He noticed, at times, that Gracie showed somewhat less enthusiasm in their sexual relationship and did not initiate often, but he attributed the change to marriage and its greater responsibilities. At times, he also sensed that she would touch him affectionately mostly in response to his touch. This included touching his face or rubbing his back. Jake saw himself as a patient and mature man who could make allowances for change. "Anyway," he reasoned, "Gracie still does nice things for me, and I know how much she respects and admires me, so this too shall pass."

Gracie's ability to be tuned into Jake was severely compromised by her low Self-Intimacy and limited Conflict Intimacy. As we have previously discussed, she had essentially decided to live two lives by maintaining the stability and comfort of her marriage and family while also moving in and out of secret infidelities.

Gracie's need for the stability of her marriage and her guilt about her infidelities kept her conscious of maintaining her overt affections with Jake. She was not faking these feelings; in fact, she did and does love him, but more than that she needs him. Because of these potent forces, Jake is none the wiser to what is going on inside Gracie and outside their marriage.

After Jake and Gracie came to counseling, Jake could admit to both himself and his wife that he had noticed subtle changes in his wife's involvement in their marriage. He noted that while the sex was always good and frequent, many times he felt Gracie was "somewhere else." While in the past he would hint at this, now because he was more aware of his own feelings (increased Self-Intimacy) and felt more able to deal with tension between them (increased Conflict Intimacy), he was able to tell Gracie that he missed how it used to feel between them. He missed feeling that she was in love with him, that she really enjoyed their sexuality—not mostly as an exercise, but as an expression of their love and mutual connection.

Jake began to see that his fear of talking about his feelings and of dealing with negative or difficult topics had led him to contribute to his and Gracie's stunted Affection Intimacy. He reasoned that if he did not tell Gracie what he wanted, needed, and experienced then he too was not being or encouraging Self-, Conflict, and Affection Intimacy.

For her part, Gracie began to recognize and take responsibility for how the denial of her early feelings of dissatisfaction and restlessness had sent her down the slippery slope of infidelity. By not admitting her feelings to herself (Self-Intimacy) and with Jake

(Conflict Intimacy), her positive, loving feelings (Affection Intimacy) toward Jake were also affected and stunted.

As Gracie began to talk with Jake about her sense of boredom and shared with him her fears, she felt more attracted to him and found herself doing more loving and affectionate things for Jake. Clearly her limited SI and CI had taken the life out of her affectionate feelings for her husband. She was relieved and encouraged to find that she could feel more in love with Jake again; she had feared that she was incapable of those feelings in a stable and loving rather than illicit relationship.

■ Samantha and Paul: An Infidelity of Loneliness

Their physical attraction had always been strong. Paul loved his wife's appearance and was very proud of her beauty. Samantha appreciated how handsome Paul was, and they both really enjoyed the physical and sexual aspects of their relationship. They also were pretty good at doing and saying sweet things for one another, at least as long as the relationship was going along easily.

However, whenever they came up against feelings of disappointment, hurt, or anger, and one or both of them withdrew in self-protection, then neither had a reliable way of reinitiating the affectionate parts of the relationship. Their limited ability to remain self-intimate in the face of their partner's resistance, combined with their previous lack of skill at staying in the tension when problems arose, resulted in the unintended attrition of their Affection Intimacy.

Because apologies were hard for both of them, this wasn't a tool they could use to repair hurt or tension. They would usually wait and then reconnect by getting involved in more perfunctory aspects of the relationship. As this pattern continued, each eventually began to be less affection intimate toward the other.

After Samantha and Paul came to therapy and began to work on the infidelity and its repercussions, they began to see how their inability to recognize and express their feelings had also hampered their ability to reconnect in affectionate ways. They both acknowledged that the only part of their Affection Intimacy that had remained intact on the outside was their sexual intimacy. And then, each admitted that they used this to gain reassurance and to soothe their own fears of abandonment. Unfortunately, neither had been able to recognize this feeling before and therefore they hadn't been able to talk about it.

Now, using the I-to-I and ESA exercises, both Samantha and Paul are finding some of the old enthusiasm and passion for their relationship. They each attribute this to digging through the difficulties that had built up between them over the years and their ability to find they could hang in there and arrive at mutually satisfying solutions. Their relationship is on the road to recovery. They still need to discover what motivated Paul's infidelity so that he can understand how and why he made this choice, and so that Samantha can gain confidence that Paul has a better way to respond to the feelings and needs that motivated the infidelity.

For now, the increased AI encourages them when they hit a rough spot in their healing and rebuilding work, and it reminds them of what originally sustained their relationship.

■ Amy and Lewis: An Infidelity of Anger

This relationship was all about passion, both positive and negative. The nonsexual and the sexual aspects of their relationship were both wonderful—sometimes even spectacular—when things were going well. But when things were bad, all bets were off. For every high in their Affection Intimacy, there was a comparable low.

Recall that both Amy and Lewis were unable to tolerate tension in the relationship, and each would assume the other was acting unloving on purpose to punish the other. Each time one of these interactions arose in their relationship, it affected everything about how they related to each other. Because this couple could not endure disappointment, their Affection Intimacy was never stable; it was always subject to the winds of change. Even during the best of times, they became less capable of being positive and loving in their words and actions. Their sexual and nonsexual physical acts of affection suffered as well.

After they began to work on Self-Intimacy and Conflict Intimacy, both began to find that there were still some sparks of loving affection buried beneath all the rage, disappointment, and anger between them. As you can imagine, the sparks of love were easily extinguished between them when the infidelities were discussed. Amy and Lewis needed much assistance to stay within the I-to-I format to contain their volatility. But with much hard work and diligence on both their parts, they began to see what part of the problem they had each contributed to the relationship. With this awareness they found themselves feeling more tender and connected to one another and were encouraged seeing they could still feel loving.

■ Cindy and Scott: Growing Pains Without Infidelity

Scott and Cindy's sexual and physical relationship was strong and satisfying for both of them. Cindy enjoyed sharing feelings and would give Scott compliments and do special things for him. Scott was not as comfortable sharing his "mushy" feelings and would even have difficulty giving Cindy compliments. He often compensated for this through Actions Affection Intimacy by initiating vacations and by following up on activities that Cindy enjoyed.

With the growth of their family and the sometimes extraordinary stresses that Scott's family of origin brought to their relationship, Cindy found herself wanting more acknowledgment from him. Unfortunately, since Scott was uncomfortable expressing feelings openly, he was not willing to do this for Cindy. Consequently, Cindy became resentful and felt less sexually responsive to Scott, less kind and caring in her words and actions, and sometimes very distant. She began avoiding holding his hand and touching him like she used to.

Scott noticed the changes in Cindy but would only bring up her withholding behaviors and complain that she was cold and punishing when he was angry about something. To retaliate, he would then withhold nonsexual physical affection and acts of kindness. He did not hold back sexually, but would instead initiate sex when matters between them were as yet unresolved. Neither knew how to get relief from this cycle.

As Cindy and Scott began to work on their Conflict Intimacy, they found to their surprise and relief that they could listen to one another, respect the other person's opinion, and eventually arrive at mutually satisfying solutions. Much of Cindy's resentment and dissatisfaction gave way to more loving and caring feelings toward Scott.

Scott found himself becoming more comfortable with a wider range of feeling—both his and Cindy's—and was relieved to learn that her expression of anger and/or unhappiness did not mean he was being chastised or necessarily blamed. With the lifting of the embargo on tough discussions he felt less encumbered, was able to give up his old defensive response of readying to defend himself, and found himself feeling safer, more comfortable, and loving toward Cindy.

What These Four Couples Teach You

Acts of affection cement our early attraction in a relationship and are often sacrificed as the relationship grows and meets typical life challenges. No one sets out to have this happen; it happens unintentionally. But as each couple became more self-aware (self-intimate) and practiced in dealing with conflict (conflict intimate), their Affection Intimacy was revitalized. As we said earlier, it takes a lot to kill love.

Of our four couples, Cindy and Scott (no infidelity) and Samantha and Paul (Infidelity of Loneliness) had the strongest Affection Intimacy foundation that helped them when they began to face their difficulties. Their mutual attraction and caring provided them with some stability and elasticity as they faced their problems head-on. In contrast, Amy and Lewis's relationship (Infidelity of Anger) is mercurial and this does not give them the resilience to harken back to a reliable and calmer time in their relationship. So, as they face their difficulties, it will take them longer to build a sense of optimism about the relationship. However, as they face the infidelity, they will have the tools for the three intimacies on hand to help them navigate the difficult and treacherous waters.

With Jake and Gracie (Infidelity of Fear), Jake's unwavering commitment to the relationship and his great Affection Intimacy will serve him well when he confronts Gracie's infidelities. Gracie's lack of passion with Jake has to be resolved and understood by her in order for her to work on herself and her behavior in the marriage. As they have begun to become more self- and conflict intimate, Gracie is beginning to feel open and alive to Jake again. As they confront the infidelities, the hard work begins in earnest.

The bond of love cemented by Affection Intimacy lays the foundation for our couples to face their eventual challenges. The early acts of affection give each couple a safety net that can catch them when they falter. However, after much time and the continued erosion of the Affection Intimacy, the net becomes worn and less elastic, and the couple can fall through. In these cases, each person's faith in the relationship and in their partner wanes, and eventually so does their motivation to make repairs.

It is interesting that Cindy and Scott face many challenges to their Affection Intimacy, yet do not choose an infidelity. We will discuss later what stops them from taking that fateful step.

Chapter Review

Affection Intimacy is the foundation of your relationship. It's the positive, loving, and caring actions that you show for your partner. These are the "gravy" of the relationship that increase and evolve when a relationship has sufficient and sustaining Self-Intimacy and Conflict Intimacy.

The four types of Affection Intimacy are: Verbal, Sexual, Actions, and Nonsexual Physical Affection Intimacy.

The Importance of Affection Intimacy

- These forms of mutual attraction and demonstrations of affection are what began the relationship and help to sustain it.

- When a couple has conflict and struggles, positive feelings and actions bolster the "glue" of the relationship, making it more resilient in the face of difficulties.

- Affection Intimacy is deepened when the partners have sufficient and growing capacities for Self-Intimacy and Conflict Intimacy. Without these, the Affection Intimacy will be threatened.

- Every couple deserves liberal doses of each of the four types of Affection Intimacy.

- Healthy fighting leads to good loving.

Recall how you expressed your affection for your partner when the relationship began and the two of you were in Sweet Symbiosis. Now consider how you expressed your affection after the disappointments of Soured Symbiosis began. Are you aware of becoming less affectionate? How did you justify this to yourself? Can you see how your diminished AI negatively affected your feelings and the relationship?

Consider how increasing your AI might affect you and your partner while realizing that it is *not* the salve that will heal the wounds in the relationship. However, AI can make working on the difficult parts easier and give one or both of you greater confidence as you proceed through the hard work.

chapter 8

the three infidelities: understanding what made your partner stray

Because people and life circumstances change over time, marriage is always a work in progress. . . . The challenge for every married couple is to stay connected . . . in spite of the inevitable kaleidoscope of change. —Judith Wallerstein and Sandra Blakeslee

Why did your partner's infidelity happen? That's the question that's been burning in your mind ever since you found out. The answer to that question always comes back to the same thing: emotions. Individuals in Long-Term Love Relationships end up betraying their partners only when they have allowed fear, loneliness, or anger to build up inside them. By not dealing with their negative emotions, people cede control to their feelings, and do what they committed not to do, betray their partners.

In this chapter we'll explain how fear, loneliness, and anger motivate infidelity, and how all infidelities are defined by the emotion that precipitated them.

HOW NEGLECTED EMOTIONS CAUSE INFIDELITY

In chapter 5 we talked about how being aware of your emotions and dealing with them in constructive ways (Self-Intimacy) is the key to individual well-being. In chapter 6 we talked about how dealing with the negative emotions between you and your partner (Conflict Intimacy) is vital to your relationship's well-being. The flip side is that if you or your partner does not pay attention to your emotions, you're inviting disaster to strike your LTLR.

Emotions Are Motivators

Have you ever wondered why we humans have emotions at all? Is it just to spice up an otherwise dull existence? No, just like every other part of us, emotions developed through evolution for a species-survival purpose.

Emotions get us to engage in external behaviors that enhance the chances of survival for ourselves and our children. For example, anger gets us to rise up and defend ourselves from threat or attack. Fear gets us to escape from danger. Jealousy gets us to protect our bond with our mate in order to enhance our offspring's chances of survival.

Our emotions motivate us to act in ways to make good feelings and their causes continue, or make bad feelings and their causes go away.

Ignore Your Negative Emotions at Your Peril

Emotions are a natural, healthy part of you. Only if you don't deal with them well do they become unhealthy. This is why the Emotional Self-Awareness Exercise that builds Self-Intimacy is so important. Being self-intimate empowers you to hear the message that your emotions are sending you, and then to act constructively in response.

For example, anxiety tells you that you are faced with a problem that you need to do something about. Once you face the problem, decide what, if anything, to do about it, and then commit to doing it, your anxiety will dissipate. The emotion served its purpose; it got you to act.

But if you ignore the anxiety and the issue that's causing it, your nervousness will grow and grow, until you either can't ignore it anymore or until the problem explodes in your face. This is why being self-intimate is so central to psychological health. If you don't listen to the messages of your emotions, especially your negative ones, all sorts of issues get worse and more complex.

And not only do our problems worsen, our negative feelings grow in intensity. When we don't allow our negative emotions healthy expression, they come out in unhealthy ways. They can negatively affect our physical health, our psychological health, and how we treat others. Instead of guiding and brightening our lives, they become toxic and cause us to act in ways that are destructive and not true to ourselves.

THE THREE EMOTIONS THAT CAUSE INFIDELITY

When fear, loneliness, or anger build up within a Long-Term Love Relationship, an extreme risk for infidelity is created. When these three emotions are allowed to grow stronger and stronger, they will very likely motivate a partner to be unfaithful.

Now, don't get us wrong. Fear, loneliness, and anger are common in every LTLR. There is nothing unhealthy about a partner feeling one or more of them at times in their relationship. And you and your LTLR will get stronger if you and your partner deal directly and constructively with any of them.

The problem arises if you or your partner is feeling fear, loneliness, or anger and ignores it, if you don't do anything constructive about the problem that is causing this emotion. Without your attention, the feeling will grow stronger and the underlying problem will get worse with time.

This set of circumstances underlies every infidelity. One of these three unattended emotions always motivates the betraying partner to be unfaithful. In order to escape their negative feelings, the betraying partner seeks to find consolation outside the relationship.

When you get to the heart of the matter, that is what an infidelity is: an attempt to run away from a painful feeling. That is what results in an Infidelity of Fear, an Infidelity of Loneliness, or an Infidelity of Anger. In the next three chapters we will describe each type of infidelity in more detail. You need to understand how each of them occur so you can make sure that one of them will never again shatter your LTLR.

Chapter Review

The timing of an infidelity is predictable. It occurs when a partner is caught in Soured Symbiosis. Whether he betrays early or later in the relationship is determined by the emotion that fuels the infidelity.

Characteristics of the Three Infidelities

- Neglected emotions lay the foundation for the betrayal.

- There are three emotions that underlie each of the types of infidelity: fear, loneliness, and anger.

At this point, can you identify which of the three emotions may have fueled your partner's infidelity? Make a note about what you assume and read on to find out what you can do to deal with this.

chapter 9

infidelity of fear: running away from old pain

> *We can't solve problems by using the same kind of thinking we used when we created them.*
> —Albert Einstein

Fear is a primal and powerful emotion. It can totally hijack your being and sweep you away or it can be a niggling little worry in the back of your mind.

Fear keeps you safe by helping you avoid danger and escape from threatening situations. We are all well served by listening to our fears. That doesn't mean you should let your fear control you, however. If you listen to it and then determine the best course of action, you have an excellent chance of doing the right thing.

Unfortunately, many of us never get good at listening to our fear. It's too threatening, too uncomfortable. So we ignore it. That's when the trouble starts.

When you disregard your fear, sometimes you end up staying too long in dangerous or destructive situations. Sometimes your fear keeps building up inside you until it gets to be so strong that it takes over your behavior, causing you to act out in the desperate attempt to escape from the feeling itself. This is the scenario played out in an Infidelity of Fear.

CHARACTERISTICS OF AN INFIDELITY OF FEAR

How do you know if the infidelity your partner had was an Infidelity of Fear? Well, it likely was if these personality traits fit your partner:

- He has low Self-Intimacy, particularly when it comes to being aware of and dealing with the emotion of fear.

- He has a long-standing, deep-seated fear of intimacy, sometimes experienced as the fear of losing himself and his independence; or of commitment, fueled by a primal fear of choosing wrongly; or of being unworthy of love.

An Infidelity of Fear results when an LTLR partner is unable or unwilling to confront these fears within himself.

If your partner had an Infidelity of Fear, it is important that you recognize that the potent combination of his fear and his tendency to ignore it predated your relationship. In fact, of the three types of infidelities, the Infidelity of Fear has the least to do with the LTLR that is betrayed and the most to do with the betraying partner's psyche and his own issues with love and intimacy.

THE FEARS THAT LEAD TO AN INFIDELITY OF FEAR

All of us want to belong and be loved. Therefore, if your partner has one of the deep-seated fears listed in the second bullet above, he is in real conflict between the desire to be in a relationship and the desire to avoid one. He will pursue relationships and for a period of time feel loved, connected, and safe, but inevitably his fears will surface. He sometimes will experience clearly defined feelings, but more often he'll only have some vague, uncomfortable notion that something isn't right.

Let's give some more detail regarding the three fears that can power an Infidelity of Fear to enable you to recognize whether your partner is struggling with one of them.

The Fear of Intimacy

The fear of intimacy is most often experienced as a reluctance to allow oneself to really get close to another person for fear of losing yourself. People caught up in this fear are concerned that the other person will take over their life; that their needs, desires, and feelings will be lost; that they will spend the rest of their lives just taking care of their partners.

This fear usually comes from having a narcissistic or self-centered parent. Such parents almost always put their needs and feelings before their child's. In this way, they teach the child that this is how intimate relationships work. So, naturally, the child grows up having a fear of closeness; he or she has learned that intimacy will just cause them hurt and disappointment because their needs won't matter.

So what does a person with this fear of intimacy do when they get into an LTLR? If his fear of intimacy is strong enough, and especially if it is reinforced by his inability to stand up for what he wants from the relationship, he will seek escape, often through an infidelity.

The Fear of Commitment

The fear of commitment is all about the fear of being wrong, of closing off possibilities. This fear comes from being continually criticized as a child for the decisions one makes, for always being told that you're wrong or that you could have done better. The person treated this way learns that he can't trust himself and his decisions, and so he becomes afraid to make them, afraid to commit to any course of action. And the bigger the decision, the more afraid he is to make it.

There are few bigger decisions than committing to an LTLR. So from the moment he enters the relationship, the commitment-phobic person has a building fear that it is a mistake. Too often he will betray his partner in order to feel less committed, to alleviate this fear.

✳ The Fear of Being Unworthy of Love

A person brings the fear of being unworthy of love into an LTLR when they were taught early on by their parents that they are unlovable. Most often this comes from parents who neglect their children, who show their kids through their inattentiveness that they don't deserve to be loved, that they aren't good enough to merit the affection that all children crave.

So the person who learned this lesson about himself goes into an LTLR "knowing" that it won't last, that your love for him will disappear once you really get to know him. This fear of an impending rejection often will cause him to act out, to escape before he is hurt, to reject you before you inevitably reject him. It will drive him to betray you.

LOW SELF-INTIMACY IS THE CATALYST

If your partner is bedeviled by any of these three fears, he is likely to feel defeated and betrayed from within. He wants nothing more than to outrun or slay these feelings. However, try as he might, he cannot get them to vanish. His limited ability to be self-intimate, that is, to acknowledge and work through the origins of the feelings, causes him to feel weak because he cannot deal with, change, or defeat them. Eventually he learns that ignoring, repressing, or denying the feelings and their impact on him brings him short-term relief.

But this type of immediate relief leads to long-term problems. There are few things more harmful to an individual's and an LTLR's health than ignoring one's fear instead of confronting it.

That is why we say that low Self-Intimacy is the catalyst of an Infidelity of Fear. Just having one of the three fears doesn't mean that your partner will inevitably stray. If he has well-developed Self-Intimacy, he can confront his fear, with your help, and overcome it. If your partner has the courage to do this, he will not be controlled by his fear.

But if he has one of these fears *and* he has low Self-Intimacy, the chances of an Infidelity of Fear resulting are very high. Low Self-Intimacy will activate his deep-seated fear, will give it power over him, will result in it controlling his behavior, and will cause him to run from his fear into another woman's arms.

INFIDELITIES OF FEAR USUALLY START EARLY ON

If your partner's infidelity started within the first few years or even the first few months of your relationship, it is most likely an Infidelity of Fear. This type of infidelity tends to occur earlier in LTLRs than Infidelities of Loneliness and Anger. This is because the underpinnings of an Infidelity of Fear, his deep-seated fear and his low Self-Intimacy that empowers it, are in place from the moment your LTLR starts.

Infidelities of Fear are also usually short-lived and not serious love affairs. This is because a person who has an Infidelity of Fear isn't looking to find love; he is looking to escape from it. So it is not uncommon for a person in this situation to have serial Infidelities of Fear over the course of his primary relationship, having one infidelity after another and sometimes more than one at a time.

BECOMING INVULNERABLE TO AN INFIDELITY OF FEAR

Of the three types of infidelity, making your Long-Term Love Relationship invulnerable to future Infidelities of Fear depends on you, the betrayed partner, the least. While you can definitely help create the necessary changes, avoiding another infidelity is much more about your partner's relationship with himself than it is about his relationship with you.

Your partner has to start by identifying and acknowledging the deep fear that is driving him. Then he has to work through it and unmask the false beliefs about himself and about love relationships that it is based on. The goal is to replace these beliefs with healthier ones. His fear will never completely disappear, but that's okay. By confronting and wrestling with it, he will become stronger and his fear will become weaker. If he has enough courage to do this work, his fear will lose the strength to control him; it will no longer have the power to drive him to betray you.

Your partner needs to include you in this process by talking with you about his fear. In this way, you can help him to overcome it. If he does not open up with you about it, this is a sure sign that he is not really confronting it, a sure sign that your LTLR is still in danger.

To get a clearer picture of this, let's look at the relationship between Gracie and Jake; they're struggling with Gracie's Infidelity of Fear.

■ Gracie and Jake: An Infidelity of Fear

Before having children, Gracie had loved Jake for who he was and because he made her feel "complete"; that is, she finally felt satisfied and no longer sought out the attention of other men. She felt content in their relationship and believed and hoped that her old insecurities had been resolved.

But after having children, Gracie found herself feeling vaguely dissatisfied and restless in the marriage. She struggled to define herself as an individual while also being a mother and wife. Gracie had few strong female role models in her family and always felt that no matter what she accomplished, her parents failed to recognize her talents. Now she feared that she was losing her separate sense of self; she felt suffocated and stifled in her new roles.

Before Gracie became involved in an infidelity, she only had a vague awareness of feelings of discomfort and discontent. However, she found herself viewing her husband in the same way she saw her father, as someone who gave conditional love based on her performance. In her marriage, this meant the role of wife and mother. Because she did not discuss these feelings with Jake or admit them to herself, she became more and more subtly distant toward him.

Gracie did not specifically look for an affair. She met Mike at work, and they often interacted on projects. Over time she found herself feeling more drawn to him. She noticed these feelings and the underlying excitement that thoughts of Mike aroused in her.

While she recognized that these feelings were not right or safe, she did nothing to examine their source and what they might mean. The excitement of her attraction toward Mike made her feel alive again. She found herself having feelings she hadn't had since the early years of her relationship with Jake.

Gracie's infidelity offered her the distraction of sex and new romance. New love and lust are the most potent antidepressants and antidotes to fear. So, as Gracie ran into an infidelity, she experienced an escape from her fear of intimacy and her feelings of discontent—or so she believed.

Despite her guilt and fear of being caught, Gracie rationalized her choice and told herself that having this affair actually made her a better wife and mother because of the needs that were now being met. She told herself that by continuing the affair, she was more capable of being the kind of wife and mother that her husband wanted.

When Jake commented that she seemed more content and attentive and less edgy and irritable toward him, Gracie let it boost her rationalization. When this rationale wore thin, she convinced herself that life without Mike would be empty because Jake was still incapable of giving her what she needed, and that the affair sustained her.

Gracie's double life lasted through her guilt, through Mike's encouragement to leave her husband, and through her weak promise to do so. Then, when Jake discovered the affair through her cell phone records, Gracie was forced to choose.

This is how Infidelities of Fear usually go: the affair will last for a period of time, and then the lover ends it because he wants to be more than a part-time person in her life or because the partner discovers the infidelity.

You, like Jake, may have been taken by complete surprise when you discovered that your partner was unfaithful. While Jake admitted later that he occasionally suspected something was different about his wife, at the time he had convinced himself that the change was innocent. Jake now is able to acknowledge that he would not allow himself to consider the worst-case scenario: an affair.

Like many couples, Jake and Gracie both worked hard to avoid recognizing and dealing with conflict and differences in their relationship, even when the tension had become palpable. To be fair to them, they lacked the skills of Self-Intimacy and Conflict Intimacy, which they desperately needed in order to get off the slippery slope of infidelity.

Unfortunately, Jake and Gracie did not learn that fight or flight is not the only option in the face of relationship tensions. They were unfamiliar as yet with how to successfully resolve changes and resolve tensions in a mutually satisfying way until they each began to work on themselves.

After Gracie and Jake sought counseling, Gracie made progress in becoming more aware of her feelings and began to recognize how she had minimized and tried to avoid the early warning signs. As the couple progressed in therapy and both shared their feelings and concerns, they became more comfortable with Conflict Intimacy and found their negative feelings being replaced by more positive feelings. If Gracie and Jake had not sought help after the discovery of the infidelity, they might have remained together, but their alliance would likely be a fragile and angry commitment.

As Jake pushed himself to acknowledge and share his intense feelings of hurt, betrayal, disappointment, and disillusionment with Gracie, he often felt overwhelmed. However, the increased Self-Intimacy he had developed helped him become more comfortable experiencing and expressing his feelings, and this skill enabled him to stay with the hurt feelings. With assistance he was able to become more conflict intimate as he calmed himself, continued to share his anger and hurt, and stayed honest with Gracie. He eventually was able to admit that at times he questioned whether he could ever trust her again and even wondered if he still loved her or even wanted to love her anymore.

While Jake was doing his part to work through the infidelity, Gracie was beginning to examine the genesis of her choice to have an affair. Gracie worked to understand the source of her early dissatisfaction and her need for constant attention. She began to recognize that her craving for attention came from her family, where her dad only noticed her when she did something extraordinary. She loved and craved this kind of attention and saw that when she was not receiving it she felt anxious, believing she would be overlooked or taken for granted.

The more Gracie explored the restless and dissatisfied feelings she had early in the marriage, the more she began to see the pattern that led to the infidelity and flirtations. As she continued to be self-intimate and acknowledge her feelings and share them with Jake, the less ignored and dissatisfied she began to feel. Jake's ability to understand her was not the key here. Instead, Gracie's willingness to see and accept herself—warts and all— signaled the turning point in her personal growth and the beginning of her being able to view commitment in a relationship as a desirable choice.

As Gracie began to recognize the feelings that motivated her infidelity, she realized that she had additional ways to cope with these feelings besides restraining and denying them or giving into them and feeling guilty.

Gracie continued to talk with Jake about the choices, feelings, and thoughts that led her to be unfaithful, even when Jake sometimes didn't want to face what was true for her. As Gracie continued to work on her ability to be conflict intimate with Jake, he began to believe that he could get past her infidelity and begin to trust her again. He felt hopeful as he watched her work in earnest to understand the infidelity's origins, sincerely accept the pain she had caused him, and remain committed to being open and honest with him.

Chapter Review

Characteristics of an Infidelity of Fear

- Your partner has low Self-Intimacy, particularly when it comes to being aware of and dealing with fear.

- Your partner has a long-standing, deep-seated fear of intimacy. This is sometimes experienced as the fear of losing himself and his independence; of commitment, fueled by a primal fear of choosing wrongly; or of being unworthy of love.

The Genesis of an Infidelity of Fear

- Low Self-Intimacy is the catalyst for an Infidelity of Fear.

- These infidelities begin early in relationships.

Becoming Invulnerable to an Infidelity of Fear

If your partner's infidelity appears to be motivated by a fear of commitment, a fear of losing his independent self in a relationship, or a fear that he is unworthy of love, then the first part of the repair work in the relationship is his. He needs to be committed to discovering which of the fears has motivated him and what the origins of that fear are.

Your work is to improve your Self-Intimacy, share your hurt with your partner, and become stronger emotionally so that you are able to listen to what he learns about what motivated his betrayal.

chapter 10

infidelity of loneliness: running toward a sense of awakening

*Much unhappiness has come into the world because
of bewilderment and things left unsaid.*
Fyodor Dostoyevsky

The one emotion that none of us feel when we're falling in love is loneliness. You miss each other when you're apart, but you don't feel lonely. Just the opposite, in fact—you feel whole, loved, and appreciated by your partner above all others.

Once you find that love, you imagine that you'll never feel lonely again. Unfortunately, all too often you do. As the months and years go by, many individuals in Long-Term Love Relationships start feeling alone again. Instead of the closeness and union they experienced at the beginning of their relationship, they feel separate, isolated, and estranged from their partner.

Sometimes when a person realizes he is feeling this way, he will try to do something about it. He'll try to talk to his partner about it, or make more time for his partner in their busy life, or be more affectionate, or be more sexual. Many times actions such as these help alleviate the problem. But often they do not.

Sometimes a person will do nothing about his loneliness, because he isn't very aware of it. If he is aware of it, he either doesn't know what to do about it or is hopeless that anything can be done to change the feeling or make it go away.

And then the loneliness gets worse.

And a lonely person, a really lonely person, is a vulnerable person. He is susceptible to the one thing that will most powerfully take his loneliness away: falling in love again. This is the very process that leads to so many affairs. These are Infidelities of Loneliness.

CHARACTERISTICS OF AN INFIDELITY OF LONELINESS

How do you determine if your partner's infidelity was such an Infidelity of Loneliness? Well, the conditions that underlie and define an Infidelity of Loneliness are:

- The development of your LTLR has been arrested at stage 2, Soured Symbiosis, by the absence of healthy Conflict Intimacy.

- Due to this low Conflict Intimacy, you and your partner have grown apart, causing deterioration in Affection Intimacy.

- This lack of closeness has become acute enough for your partner that he feels alone and unloved.

- Your partner has low Self-Intimacy.

Similar to an Infidelity of Fear, low Self-Intimacy in your partner plays a role in the process that leads to an Infidelity of Loneliness. But unlike Infidelities of Fear, here the key is that your relationship's low Conflict Intimacy has led to the creation of real distance and loneliness between you. Sadly, this was the fertile ground from which your partner's Infidelity of Loneliness sprang.

Yes, you had a role in creating this situation, but we want to remind you that you are not responsible for your partner betraying you and your relationship. You did not drive him to make this painful mistake. He didn't have to respond to his loneliness by having an affair.

Low Conflict Intimacy Leads to Loneliness

So how did this happen? How can it be that a man who once so loved you betrayed you with another because he no longer felt close to you?

Well, it's all about Conflict Intimacy. The closeness, the warmth, and the love in our Long-Term Love Relationships are more fragile than we think. That Affection Intimacy, which so deliciously dominated your relationship at the beginning, doesn't last forever without help.

That help, strangely enough, comes from fighting. If you fight well you will love well. Fighting well means both you and your partner bringing up your negative feelings, confronting them, and working through them together. This openness, honesty, and respect for each other's feelings brings you closer and defines healthy Conflict Intimacy.

But when you don't fight well, your love starts to get submerged by a growing undertow of unspoken disappointments and differences. This sea of negative emotions creates a gulf between you and your partner; eventually you're standing on opposite shores, growing farther and farther apart from each other. You don't feel the warmth and closeness you used to feel. You're not in contact with him anymore. Your day-to-day life feels like a series of automatic and lifeless transactions. Instead of feeling close, intimate, and loving with your partner, you feel distant and isolated. If you don't do something about this, your loneliness begins to consume and eventually control your life.

Such loneliness is reversible. If your partner had the Self-Intimacy to be consciously aware of his loneliness and then talked with you about it honestly and clearly, you two would have had a chance to heal your LTLR before he had an infidelity. You could have openly dealt with your differences and your accumulated hurts and disappointments. You could have developed Conflict Intimacy, either on your own or with the help of a couples therapist.

A SLOW PROCESS

But if your partner has had an Infidelity of Loneliness, the two of you were not successful in developing Conflict Intimacy. And so his loneliness continued to grow. Usually this is a slow, insidious process, marked by the attrition of the betraying partner's faith in the capacity of the LTLR to be successful, to take care of his need for love and intimacy. Your partner missed what you two used to have and he did not know how to get it back. Worse, he doubted whether you could get it back at all.

Unlike Infidelities of Fear, Infidelities of Loneliness do not usually occur at the beginning of a Long-Term Love Relationship. Because it takes time for loneliness to overtake love, Infidelities of Loneliness typically take place five to seven years into the relationship.

Individuals who have an Infidelity of Loneliness generally do not seek out an infidelity. In fact, they are often largely unaware of the depth of their loneliness. This is an example of low Self-Intimacy in action. Out of touch with their feelings, people in this situation are surprised by their mounting attraction for another.

The Seductive Antidote

At first, when he finds himself drawn to another person, such an individual is likely to minimize the attraction, to chalk it up to being married for so long or to long work hours, or to label it as just a temporary, passing feeling. But the attraction is very seductive. He suddenly feels alive in a way he hasn't for years. This stands in strong contrast to how emotionally shut down he has been in his primary relationship.

When you add this new sense of aliveness to the betraying partner's low Self-Intimacy and his LTLR's low Conflict Intimacy, you can see how an Infidelity of Loneliness is a great threat to his relationship. The betraying partner believes he is in love, a new kind of love that he has never experienced before, to replace the love that can never be regained between him and his partner.

But this is a mirage. His infidelity relationship is built on Need Love. All it does is temporarily mask his loneliness. The affair is fueled and fed by his infidelity partner meeting his need to not feel lonely; it doesn't have a lot to do with loving who she is. As a result, these relationships rarely last.

BECOMING INVULNERABLE TO AN INFIDELITY OF LONELINESS

As with any of the three types of infidelities, the first step in making your LTLR invulnerable to an Infidelity of Loneliness reoccurring in the future is truly healing from this betrayal. As we discussed in detail in chapter 1, this involves working through your terrible pain, anger, and fear as well as your partner earning your trust back over time.

At the same time, you and your partner have to address head-on the two factors that led to his betrayal. First is his low Self-Intimacy, which allowed his loneliness to grow unchecked so that it came to overtake and control him, leading to the infidelity. Your partner absolutely must commit to work on building up his SI, not only so that he becomes highly aware of the emotions he is feeling, but also so that he is then able to talk with you about them, whether good or bad. If he does not do this, another Infidelity of Loneliness will likely occur in the future.

Second, you and he have to address the low Conflict Intimacy that led to the distance between you. This is what gave birth to the loneliness that enabled his infidelity. The gap can absolutely be closed, but you both need to work on this, primarily by focusing on dealing with your differences.

A mountain of hurt, disappointment, and resentment has piled up between the two of you. These negative feelings have to be dealt with. They're like germs infecting a wound; in order for you to heal your relationship and become close, intimate, and loving again, you have to clean out the wound. This is where CI is key. Learning to fight well will enable you to work past these negative emotions so you can let go of them. Once you do that, we promise that you will find your loving, affectionate feelings for each other returning.

After all, that's the real antidote to loneliness: finding that the person you fell in love with is still there and still loves you. That is the discovery you make once you learn how to deal with the inevitable differences and conflicts that any two people will have. You're still the same people who fell in love and wanted to spend the rest of their lives together. Learn to fight well with each other and you will find your love reemerging and the loneliness that plagued your relationship melting away.

■ Samantha and Paul: An Infidelity of Loneliness

After having three children, Samantha and Paul's lack of resolution over money issues, the lessening demonstrations of affection, and their repeated inability to resolve certain arguments had caused them to feel less close and therefore to have less enthusiasm about the relationship.

Their arguments usually ended with angry words of accusation. Their conflicts hardly ever reached any satisfactory resolution. Instead they've each found themselves in a state of utter exhaustion, too spent to devote much energy to keeping up the argument. This has gotten so unpleasant that they don't even bother; they've fallen into a Conflict Avoidant pattern of relating.

So why and how did Paul take the step across the boundary of his marriage into infidelity? It was a slow process that just crept up on him. As the couple failed to resolve any of their issues, their negative feelings affected their ability and willingness to be affection intimate with each other. Paul found his anger and disappointment with Samantha diminishing his desire to be sexual and act in caring ways toward his wife. Then, at times, he would be desperate to normalize their relationship and he would initiate sexual contact. For her part, Samantha often felt alone and separate in the relationship. But she too did not know how to break their impasse.

Paul prided himself on being a good husband, father, and employee. He always knew the boundaries for work and personal relationships and never came close to crossing them. Initially, there was nothing special about his interaction with Mary at work. However, after working with her for more than a year, he found that his thoughts often included her, and that he would look forward to seeing her at the office. He also found himself finding excuses to come into contact with her. He began to examine these feelings and realized that he came alive in her presence.

At first he told himself that this feeling was quite innocent and would pass. Of course, it didn't, and he began to sense from her a mutual attraction. At this point, he was not actively seeking an affair, yet he was beginning to experience the attraction as intoxicating.

It was this intense attraction that eventually convinced him that something significant was missing in his marriage. These exciting feelings contrasted sharply with how deadened he felt with Samantha. Unfortunately, Paul lacked the insight to know that his and Samantha's inability to deal with conflict well was the cause of their emotionally flat relationship. Unbeknownst to him, he had put his positive feelings on hold in his marriage. That had led to a deepening crisis of loneliness for him, which resulted in the electric attraction he suddenly felt for Mary.

That sense of coming back to life was liberating, frightening, and eventually undeniable. Paul gradually chose to become more emotionally involved with Mary. They began to talk about their personal lives, and both of them felt something was missing in their primary relationships.

As the emotional connection between them grew, the sexual attraction became more charged. Even as Paul crossed the fidelity line and became physically intimate with Mary, he was conflicted. He found his affection and desire for Mary irresistible but also felt guilty that he had betrayed Samantha. He loved Samantha but questioned whether he was "in love" with her. With the new feelings for Mary, he now was able to see how far apart he and Samantha had grown.

Infidelities of Loneliness are usually discovered by the betrayed partner, as was the case with Samantha and Paul. While Samantha did not want to acknowledge what she suspected, the change in Paul was too obvious to ignore. She confronted him and while he denied an affair, Samantha soon was able to piece together evidence of the relationship that he could not contradict. When confronted by Samantha, Paul actually felt relieved to be out from under the lies and deceit, as well as petrified that a decision had to be made. Paul chose to end the relationship with Mary and get into marital counseling with Samantha.

For three months the couple has been working successfully on becoming both more self-intimate and conflict intimate. Each has begun to feel some of the old spark of love they once had; now, as Samantha feels emotionally stronger, she is asking Paul to explain how and why he got into an affair with Mary. This request by Samantha is normal, yet as the couple attempts to dig into this topic, each of them struggles to maintain gains they have each made in both self-intimaty and conflict intimacy.

Paul, however, does not want to hurt Samantha with some of the truth about how much in love he was with Mary. Samantha, to her credit, is able to stay in the role of Inquirer and tells Paul that she will do her best to remain calm, open to his feelings, and to ask helpful questions (goal 8, Inquirere role, Maturity Goals Handout).

Paul begins to describe to Samantha how unaware he had been that he had partially given up on their marriage ever improving. He admits that while he was not ever thinking about ending the marriage, he realizes in retrospect that he had lowered his standard for what a happy marriage is. It was only when he found himself captivated by Mary that he began to realize that something inside of him had been turned off or felt dead. This was hard for Samantha to hear, but as she pushed herself to remember that Paul was describing his experience, she began to have a clearer picture of what their marriage had become for him. As she later thought about his experience, she realized there was truth in it for her as well—she too had been blind to her feelings of dissatisfaction.

As Samantha listened to Paul describe his feelings about Mary, she also asked him questions to help him explore more of what he felt and thought. This was a double-edged sword for her—hearing about him coming alive with someone else coupled with the knowledge that the more he understood about what motivated the infidelity, the more confident she could be that he was committed to change. Motivated by new hope, she continued to challenge herself to hear Paul's experience.

With Samantha's assistance and his hard work, Paul realized how out of touch he had been with his disappointment, anger, and resignation over the course of the marriage. He began to pinpoint when he had lowered his expectations and was able to identify the cascade effect this had on him and the marriage. He could see that as he expected less of the relationship he gave less, avoiding the growing gulf between them and withdrawing more. He realized how this lack of Self-Intimacy bled into his inability to handle the growing conflicts.

Paul worked diligently to acknowledge and express his positive and negative feelings with Samantha. She did the same, especially as she realized how she too had become complacent and Conflict Avoidant in the relationship. As Paul recognized how he made himself vulnerable to an infidelity, he remained committed to being self-intimate and promised Samantha that he would share his feelings with her, especially if he found himself attracted to someone else again. She appreciated knowing this and promised to be just as honest. They each agreed to not avoid uncomfortable conversations, no matter what the topic.

Chapter Review

Characteristics of an Infidelity of Loneliness

- The development of your LTLR has been arrested at stage 2, Soured Symbiosis, by the absence of healthy Conflict Intimacy.

- Due to this low Conflict Intimacy, you and your partner have grown apart, causing deterioration in Affection Intimacy.

- This lack of closeness has become acute enough for your partner that he feels alone and unloved.

- Your partner has low Self-Intimacy.

The Genesis of an Infidelity of Loneliness

- Low Conflict Intimacy is the catalyst.

- Low Self-Intimacy follows.

- These infidelities begin later in a relationship.

- The infidelity is the antidote to feeling lonely.

- The infidelity is based on Need Love.

Becoming Invulnerable to an Infidelity of Loneliness
If your partner's infidelity is one of Loneliness, then his work is to commit to examining the feelings behind his loneliness—to understand what led to his becoming so emotionally flat. He will also have to be willing to give up the affair. Of all the infidelities, this is the one most challenged by the "other woman," as your partner often truly feels love for her.

Your work is to increase your Self-Intimacy and talk about your hurt and devastation without blaming. As you gain emotional strength you will be ready to hear about how your partner began to lose his feelings for you. This strength will increase your capacity to be conflict intimate as you then listen to him describe how alive he felt in the affair.

You will have to remind yourself that before you can begin to regain trust in him, you have to see that he understands how he made the choice to be unfaithful and how you felt as the relationship slowly eroded over time.

chapter 11

infidelity of anger: running for revenge

> *If passion drives you, let reason hold the reins.*
> —Benjamin Franklin

Anger may very well be the most misunderstood emotion. It's thought of as something "bad" that causes people to do mean things, when actually, anger is as natural and healthy and normal as any other emotion. In fact, anger can be a very positive force in a person's life, causing them to stand up against injustice or to fight to protect what is dear to them.

If there is one thing about anger that everyone would agree on, it is that, like fear, anger is a very primal and powerful emotion. In the blink of an eye, it can sweep us away, taking over our mind and body, causing us to "see red." That's why anger gets a bad rap. Most of us allow our anger to control us at times, resulting in actions that we later regret. But anger itself isn't the problem. The blame lies with our inability to control it.

When anger builds up inside and isn't dealt with, people can lash out at almost anything. When something triggers their anger, they lose control of it and overreact. They end up wanting to hurt the person who is hurting them.

Handling anger like this is unhealthy for all LTLRs. When one partner has a history of not being able to deal with his anger well, and then builds up more hurt from within the relationship, his anger will come to control him. He starts wanting to hurt the one he loves. And there is no more effective way to do this than by having an infidelity. This is what leads to Infidelities of Anger.

CHARACTERISTICS OF AN INFIDELITY OF ANGER

Was your partner's betrayal fueled by revenge and anger? See if the following characteristics fit your partner and your LTLR:

- Your partner has low Self-Intimacy, particularly when it comes to dealing with situations in which he feels hurt or disappointed.

- Consequently, your partner has a great deal of hurt and disappointment built up inside, which in turn creates the buildup of anger.

- There is low Conflict Intimacy in your LTLR, defined by either a strong Hostile Dependent style or a strong Conflict Avoidant style of handling your differences.

- Consequently, more and more hurt, disappointment, and then anger have built up in your partner, feelings that he has failed to deal with in any healthy way. So his anger controls him, finally causing him to betray you.

Low Self-Intimacy and Conflict Intimacy are equal partners in creating the conditions that lead to an Infidelity of Anger. The inability of your partner to deal in a healthy way with anger, both within himself and in his relationship with you, is the key here.

How Anger Took Over Your Partner

Of course, earlier in your relationship, your partner's love for you was stronger than his anger. He was caring, not mean; kind, not hurtful. So what happened? How did he get to this point?

Well, for almost all partners who engage in an Infidelity of Anger, the seeds of the betrayal predate the LTLR. Your partner most likely came into your relationship with a history of not dealing with conflict well. We're talking here about real conflict, conflict with emotional undertones, conflict causing true hurt, disappointment, and anger.

Thus your partner entered your relationship already having negative feelings festering within him. Once these existing feelings were coupled with any new negative ones that arose in your relationship, your partner became consumed with anger.

At this point, his anger developed enough emotional power to take over his behavior and cause him to believe that his infidelity was justified by your mistreatment or misunderstanding of him. He then acted out of a desire for revenge.

LOW SELF-INTIMACY

Everyone feels and lashes out in anger every now and then. But there's a difference between this normal angry reaction and people who have real trouble controlling their anger. People who are unable to contain their anger deny or repress their hurts and disappointments. Hurt and disappointment are the emotions that fuel anger.

So the key to dealing with anger is paying attention when you feel hurt and/or disappointed, and then doing what you have to do to work through those painful feelings. You have to be self-intimate enough to know when these emotions are present within you and be able to act on that awareness.

But partners who have Infidelities of Anger never developed this ability. This is especially common in men because they are trained by our culture that acknowledging, to themselves or to others, that they are feeling hurt is weak, not manly. The opposite is actually true: to acknowledge one's hurt is an act of strength. It takes courage to admit such vulnerability. Denying it is an act of fear, done out of weakness. But that is not what our culture teaches, particularly to our men.

So if your partner has had an Infidelity of Anger, the roots of his betrayal stretch back to before you were in his life, to his failure to ever learn to face his hurt feelings. Because he never developed Self-Intimacy skills, negative feelings built up inside his psyche, and the hurt and disappointment fueled more and more anger within him.

TOXIC CONFLICT STYLE

While a history of low Self-Intimacy is one of the factors that leads to the possibility of your partner engaging in an Infidelity of Anger, the trigger is almost always low Conflict Intimacy. The additional deep hurt, disappointment, and anger that develops in your LTLR puts him over the edge to the point that his anger controls his behavior.

In your LTLR, this low Conflict Intimacy can take one of two forms, as we described in chapter 6, Hostile Dependence or Conflict Avoidance. In both of these styles, as conflict is not dealt with constructively, anger builds and can take over one of the partners. This can result in a number of different things. Your partner could start acting coldly toward you. He could make little digs. He could start ignoring you. He could act passive-aggressively, doing annoying little things.

Or he could start having an infidelity. Sometimes he will even convince himself that the infidelity is his due for the hurts and disappointments that you have "inflicted" on him. But if his low Self-Intimacy history around hurt, disappointment, and anger collides with your LTLR's low Conflict Intimacy, it's often only a matter of time before he betrays you in an Infidelity of Anger.

THE TIMING AND UNMASKING OF THE INFIDELITY

Unlike the other two types of infidelities, an Infidelity of Anger is just as likely to occur early in a Long-Term Love Relationship as late. It all depends on how much hurt, disappointment, and anger your partner brings into your LTLR. Some partners come into an LTLR with so much pent-up pain that it takes very little negative feelings in the relationship to trigger their anger and the desire for revenge. Often a partner holds unresolved rage toward a previous lover, which then gets taken out on you.

If the built-up pain isn't as great, the repeated disappointments in your LTLR will fuel an Infidelity of Anger. When this is the case, the infidelity happens after a number of years in the LTLR, sometimes more than five or ten years.

Whenever it happens, one commonality to Infidelities of Anger is that the betraying partner often wants to be found out. He probably won't consciously be aware of this and he won't knowingly leave clues, but leave hints he will. For it's only when he is found out that his revenge is taken; it's only when you discover his infidelity that he is able to get back at you for the pain that he blames you for.

Of course, you're not to blame for his pain; his feelings are his responsibility. You have a role in the low Conflict Intimacy in the LTLR, but you didn't force him not to deal with his pain and anger, and you're not responsible for the feelings carried along from his past. But if he had an Infidelity of Anger, he does blame you and he does want revenge. That's why he will leave bread crumbs for you to follow and uncover the betrayal.

BECOMING INVULNERABLE TO AN INFIDELITY OF ANGER

Much like with an Infidelity of Loneliness, after doing the difficult work to heal from the pain and trauma of the betrayal, the keys to making sure this never happens again center around your partner overcoming his low Self-Intimacy and the two of you developing your Conflict Intimacy.

Your partner must commit to work on growing his Self-Intimacy, especially in regard to how he handles hurt and disappointment as well as anger. He must develop his in-the-moment awareness of these emotions and then practice talking with you constructively, in a non-blaming way, about them.

In addition, he must do the hard work necessary to identify and work through the pain and anger he has built up from his past. Only after this will he be safe from being hijacked by his anger in the future. Only then will the danger of his anger controlling him, causing him to act out for revenge, be eliminated.

And you and he together have to work on developing the Conflict Intimacy in your relationship. You cannot afford to continue dealing with conflict in either the Hostile Dependent or the Conflict Avoidant style. You both have to learn to solve your differences as a team, not approaching them in an attacking, defensive way and not brushing them under the rug. You must deal with conflict openly and constructively, with each of you taking responsibility for your part in the problems and each of you expressing caring and regret for the pain you have caused your partner.

When you and your partner have done these things, anger will no longer have the power to take over your Long-Term Love Relationship and cause an Infidelity of Anger.

■ Amy and Lewis:
An Infidelity of Anger

Amy and Lewis have been together for fifteen passionate and long years. When things were good, they were very, very good, and when they were bad, they were awful. Their compatibility was challenged since early in their courtship when their differences emerged. Each had tried to rationalize, minimize, blame, or change the other person, but to no avail.

Lewis also grew up observing his parents' unresolved mutual frustrations and resentments toward one another. His parents were poorly matched but seemed resigned to remaining married. When he met Amy, he felt alive and excited about their passion, a wonderful antidote to the dull lifelessness that existed between his parents. However, as he encountered normal and inevitable feelings of disappointment in the relationship, he did not know that they did not mean that something was seriously wrong. Without this knowledge and the tools necessary to resolve the disappointment, he began to feel hurt and angry and started to believe that their love and commitment were threatened.

Early in the relationship when Lewis tried to talk with Amy about his disappointed feelings, he came across as defensive, critical, and attacking. Amy reacted by defending herself and didn't know how to bridge Lewis's frustrations. Lewis eventually found his disappointments, frustrations, and hurts being replaced by more potent and toxic feelings of anger.

As the cycle of unresolved conflict continued, Lewis convinced himself that his anger and dissatisfaction toward Amy were justified and unavoidable. As opportunities arose at work and recreation, he chose to become involved with numerous women. Some of these liaisons were short-lived, mostly sexual in nature, and some were both sexual and romantic. He admitted that he was an opportunist who found that women were often readily available.

Amy and Lewis sought counseling when Amy discovered the infidelities and she could no longer tolerate both the pain of the betrayal and their continued cycle of Hostile Dependence. Counseling has helped each of them to slowly become more self-intimate and conflict intimate. They have each made progress. While in the past Amy would vacillate between trying to keep the peace and exploding at Lewis with her pent-up frustrations and anger, now she is able to identify her feelings, ask him for a good time to talk, and then share with him what she is feeling without blaming him. Lewis, in turn, has been able to see the pain he has caused Amy and understand that her feelings are about her experience and not an indictment or necessarily a description of him.

As they are able to listen and share there is less toxic anger being expressed between them.

They are beginning to talk about the impact that the infidelities have had on the relationship as well as explore what led Lewis to choose to be unfaithful. As Amy asks more questions regarding the details around the infidelities, it is a struggle for her to listen and not react, but she has made enough progress to be able to productively stay in the conversation a little longer each time.

Sharing the details of his betrayals was not something Lewis was comfortable with either. Being honest with himself and Amy were not the norm for him. He worked with great effort to be honest and to fight his internal desire to stop the conversation because he didn't like hearing who he has been and seeing how he has acted. It took more than a month of continued asking and sharing in order for Lewis to admit to Amy and himself the number of infidelities he had had during the marriage. Nevertheless, Lewis persevered.

As Lewis continued to be self- and conflict intimate, describing for Amy the anger and frustrations he felt early in the relationship, he also admitted that he took any slights that he perceived from her as intentional. Unfortunately for Lewis, feeling criticized and blamed and expecting to be abandoned or punished were normal for him when he was growing up. He recognized that the seeds of his infidelity were sown both in his early family experience and early in their LTLR.

In the past Lewis could not have admitted that he chose to be unfaithful. He would have defended his actions as being Amy's fault, claiming that she drove him to it. But now he was examining the feelings that motivated his choices. He came to see that he had not been looking for love, but more for the attention, an ego boost, and a passive way to retaliate for the hurts he felt Amy had inflicted on him.

Of our three couples dealing with infidelity, Amy and Lewis may have the most difficult path back to intimacy after an infidelity. Their relationship has never had a solid foundation of trust or a means to work through their differences. Much effort is required from each of them, individually and as a couple, but as you can see, they are each willing to make the sustained effort.

Lewis is doing his part to increase his Self-Intimacy and Conflict Intimacy as well as examining the genesis of his anger in both his family and the relationship. Amy is developing the ability to listen to the truth from Lewis in spite of how hard it is to hear and acknowledge. They are both working diligently to stay out of a Hostile Dependent cycle of relating.

In addition to healing from the disappointment and hurt of the betrayals, Amy is challenging herself to examine why she has been willing to accept so little in the relationship. She also is finding ways to express her feelings and needs that are more direct and is learning that she does not need Lewis's agreement in order to feel okay about a belief or feelings she has. And lastly, both she and Lewis have begun to find more emotionally mature ways to deal with inevitable relationship conflict.

As they make personal and relationship progress, they continue to report that some of their early feelings of love, lust, and like are returning. Most recently, each has said that they feel more connected, optimistic, and stable both personally and in the marriage than they have probably ever felt.

Chapter Review

Characteristics of an Infidelity of Anger

- Your partner has low Self-Intimacy, particularly when it comes to dealing with situations in which he feels hurt or disappointed.

- Consequently, your partner has a great deal of hurt and disappointment built up inside, which in turn creates the buildup of anger.

- There is low Conflict Intimacy in your LTLR, defined by either a strong Hostile Dependent style or a strong Conflict Avoidant style of handling your differences.

- Consequently, more and more hurt, disappointment, and then anger have built up in your partner, feelings that he has failed to deal with in any healthy way. So his anger controls him, finally causing him to betray you.

Low Self-Intimacy and Conflict Intimacy are equal partners in creating the conditions that lead to an Infidelity of Anger. The inability of your partner to deal in a healthy way with anger, both within himself and in his relationship with you, is the key here.

The Genesis of an Infidelity of Anger

- Low Self-Intimacy

- Low Conflict Intimacy

- Vacillating Affection Intimacy

- Seeds of infidelity predate the relationship

Becoming Invulnerable to an Infidelity of Anger

If your partner's infidelity is one motivated by anger, then the steps you will need to take include:

- Changing your toxic conflict style: Hostile Dependent or Conflict Avoidant

- Your partner committing to working on his Self-Intimacy

- His identifying the sources of his anger within his early experiences and in your relationship

- You and he both increasing your Conflict Intimacy skills

chapter 12

healing your relationship: instructions for both of you

Where love rules, there is no will to power;
and where power predominates, there love is
lacking. The one is the shadow of the other.
—Carl Jung

Now that the unthinkable has happened, what do you do? Your heart has been torn asunder by your partner's betrayal. But you still love him. He says he still loves you. He says he doesn't want to lose you, that he's willing to do anything to save your Long-Term Love Relationship.

So you've decided to give him a second chance, to give the two of you a second chance. It's a risky move, a scary decision, but you think the love you shared is worth it. You don't want to give up on the dreams you had for your relationship. You believe there's a chance he won't betray you again, a chance you will be able to trust him again. You think the two of you might be able to get the love and closeness back again.

But how do you do this? How do you go from this awful place of excruciating pain, terrible rage, and shattered trust to the promised land of abiding love and total confidence? Believe us, it can be done. It's at times very painful and other times pretty scary, but it's actually not all that complicated.

There are two tasks in this process: working through your deep hurt, disappointment, rage, and other negative feelings; and rebuilding your ability to trust your partner.

In this chapter, we will teach you how to accomplish these goals and heal the wound of the infidelity. This is the first step toward ensuring that an infidelity never shatters your LTLR again.

TASK NUMBER ONE: GETTING PAST THE PAIN AND THE ANGER

Dealing with the reality of finding out that your lover has betrayed you is in some ways akin to facing the death of a loved one. In fact, sometimes it feels like someone, or something, has died. And just like the mourning process, processing your partner's infidelity is defined by the deep, painful feelings you are experiencing. In order to get past the betrayal, as in coming to terms with the passing of someone you loved, you have to work through these raw emotions.

For the Partner Who Was Betrayed

As the person who has just had her heart broken by your partner's infidelity, you have a choice to make: whether safety becomes your top priority. Because you're in excruciating pain, part of you is screaming out to do anything to make the hurt go away, and, above all else, to not let yourself be hurt any more than you already have been. Seemingly, the best way to do this is to use your hurt and anger to protect yourself and to lash out at him.

Many people in your situation give in to the seductive pull of this desperate cry for safety. The problem is that if you put safety first, you may be safer, but you will be alone. There is no way that your LTLR will have any possibility of healing if you let your fear control you. Not only that, but walling yourself off with your pain rather than working through it also reduces the chance that you'll ever be successful in an LTLR.

So you need to act with courage in the face of your heart-break. Do not let the fear of exposing your heart to the person who has just broken it stop you from doing it. Letting yourself be vulnerable like this sounds crazy, but it is not. It is the only way for you to get past the pain, to not have it dominate your life anymore. And it is the only way that your Long-Term Love Relationship will have a chance to heal.

Using the ESA Exercise

So once you've decided to act with courage and deal with your aching emotions, what do you do? Your first step is to take an inventory of your feelings. You must be experiencing some combination of deep hurt, sadness, loss, fear, humiliation, and anger. And what about inadequacy or even a sense of guilt? Use the Emotional Self-Awareness (ESA) Exercise as detailed in chapter 5 to figure out exactly what emotions you're feeling, how strongly you're feeling them, and precisely what about the infidelity is causing you to feel them.

Write down your answers to the ESA questions; writing often helps us make sense of our emotions, especially when they're so strong. Remember, there will be multiple reasons why you are feeling some of these emotions. For example, you may feel enraged not only because he betrayed you, but also because he lied to you about it, and also because he took her to your favorite romantic resort. Or you may feel humiliated not only because he picked somebody twenty years younger than you, but also because everyone at his work knows about her. Or you may be afraid he's going to leave you for her, you may fear that he doesn't love you anymore, while at the same time fearing that leaving him might be best for you, even though you don't know if you can handle being alone.

In any traumatic situation like this, your first responsibility is to take good care of yourself and you can't do that unless you know what you're feeling and why. And don't be surprised, in spite of the awful thing he's done, when you find yourself feeling love and even longing and desire for him. Just because you're so hurt and enraged doesn't mean that you don't love him anymore. Sometimes betrayed partners find themselves desiring their unfaithful partner a lot more after they find out about an infidelity and can't get enough of them sexually. So take a clear, hard look at your feelings, in all their strength, whatever their causes and however contradictory some of them may seem. Having the courage to face your pain is the first step in getting past it. Owning your feelings, identifying them and their causes, leads you to understanding and having compassion for yourself. This is the major first step in working through the trauma of the betrayal.

Once you have a good understanding of your current matrix of emotions, you're ready for the next step: starting to actively, constructively express them to your partner and to others you are close to.

Using the I-to-I Exercise

How do you talk about the betrayal in a way that is ultimately constructive for the relationship? No doubt you've already been talking about it, or should we say yelling, arguing, accusing, and pleading? Obviously, it's very difficult to discuss the infidelity without the interaction devolving into attacking and defending.

We recommend that you and your partner agree to spend time talking about the infidelity within the structure of the I-to-I exercise (as detailed in chapter 6). This doesn't mean one conversation, but a series of discussions using this format.

In a number of these conversations, you will be the Initiator, talking about your emotions surrounding the betrayal: your deep hurt, sadness, fear, anger, and so on. You will express what you've learned through the ESA exercise about what you're feeling and what is causing you to feel that way. You will really let the pain and the rage pour out of you, as an expression of your experience rather than as a payback to your partner. The more you express the range of your feelings and experiences, the more quickly you'll be able to get past the betrayal. This is especially true if your partner fulfills the Inquirer role well and lets you express yourself without getting defensive, and if he is able to show real remorse for the pain he's caused you. Make sure you don't attack him, no matter how much you want to. Your job is to talk about yourself, your feelings, and your problems with what he's done.

Also use the I-to-I exercise to get your questions answered about the infidelity. Everyone in an LTLR who has been betrayed through an infidelity is caught in a trap: Part of them is obsessed with finding out the details of the infidelity. They can't get their questions about it out of their head. At the same time, they are afraid to find out the details, afraid to know what it was really like. So you're not alone in these contradictory feelings.

You can ask your partner to be the Initiator and tell you about his infidelity, but be warned: only ask questions that you are ready to have answered. Remind yourself that the answers you seek may be very painful. Will knowing them really help you move on? For some people, learning the facts does help them make sense of what happened and get past it. For others, the intimate details just increase their pain. So be careful; don't let your curiosity control you. Ask for information that you think will lead you toward understanding and resolution, and not for details that will only deepen your hurt and rage.

For the Partner Who Strayed

The assumption for the partner who was unfaithful is that you have ended your relationship with the other woman, realized it was a mistake, still truly love your partner, and want to make your Long-Term Love Relationship with her work.

With that being the case, there is no question that while your partner is in terrible pain right now and justifiably very angry, this is a tough time for you as well. You're having to take responsibility for breaking your solemn commitment to your partner and hurting her in just about the worst way possible. She's lost all trust in you; you see her suffering and know that you're the cause. She's very likely lashing out at you and you know that she has every reason to do so.

Before very long, men in your position just want it to be over. You want her to get past it, let it go, realize that she can trust you again. After all, you've told her that you're really sorry and that you will never stray again. Why won't she get over it?

Well, be careful what you ask for. Sometimes a betrayed partner will "get over it" quickly, in a few days or a few weeks. But when this happens, they haven't really healed. They're just burying their pain and anger out of fear, fear of losing you. Those buried negative feelings will resurface and poison the relationship going forward. So while in the short term it's a relief for you if she seems to be ready to move on quickly, it will come back to haunt you and your relationship over and over again.

Using the I-to-I Exercise

What you need to do now is be there for your partner by helping her express her feelings about your betrayal. This is no fun for you, but you need to encourage it. You need to allow your partner to get her hurt out and you need to take her anger without getting defensive and without trying to mute her. The more you can listen to her with understanding, the more quickly she'll be able to put these feelings behind her. This will take weeks or months, but as time goes on you'll see that the rawness of her anguish and anger, and the frequency that she talks about them, will diminish if you keep listening, validating, and expressing your regret.

If you join with her in working within the structure of the I-to-I exercise, this process will be hastened along. As the Inquirer, help her express her feelings by reflecting them back to her and by asking her questions about them. At times, it will be tough for you not to get defensive, but this is key. She doesn't have a right to beat you up or hurt you back with her anger, but she does have every right to feel it. You need to be strong enough to help her get it out by listening and understanding.

Using the ESA Exercise

You also will be well served to be open and honest with her when she asks for information about the infidelity. There will likely be times when she presses you for exacting, intimate details, including about sex. Whatever you do, do not lie to her. You don't have to answer every question right away. If you think an answer will only have destructive consequences, put her off; ask her to think about why she's asking and what good knowing the answer will do. A good rule of thumb is that questions are valid if they relate more to the relationship between the two of you than about the infidelity. There's a big difference between "Was sex better with her?" and "Was there something about the sex with her that was missing in our relationship?"

She's also going to ask you the "Why?" question. In order to really answer it you have to know yourself. Use the ESA exercise (chapter 5) to get a deeper understanding of your feelings and what caused them. Find out whether it was fear, loneliness, or anger that led you to be unfaithful. Be honest with your partner about what you felt and why before, during, and after the infidelity. And use the ESA exercise to get in touch with and then talk with her about your love for her, why you aren't giving up on the two of you, and what your commitment is to her.

She very understandably needs a great deal of reassurance of your love for her. You can help her get her confidence in your love back through your words and deeds, like being there for her when she needs to talk, again and again, about her pain or about her anger at you.

TASK NUMBER TWO: REBUILDING THE TRUST

Your trust in your partner was shattered in an instant. It will take a long time to get it back—months, if not years. And there is only one way to build trust. Words, no matter how good, won't do it; they simply aren't enough. Actions are what's necessary. Your partner not only has to talk the talk, but walk the walk. That is, he has to be scrupulous about doing what he says he is going to do and hide nothing. If he does this, while at the same time helping you work through your pain and anger, then you are going to be faced with a difficult decision: should you let yourself trust him again?

You don't know how much of your past together was a lie. You feel like a fool because you did trust him. Now you don't know if you can trust a word he says. How you wish you could trust him again, but you can't, indeed you shouldn't. He has to bend over backward to deserve it again.

But no matter what he does, he can't earn your trust back if you don't help. First, together you have to devise ways for him to show you that he is indeed trustworthy and true. And then if he does those things, repeatedly, without fail, over time, you have to choose whether or not to trust him again.

A List of Trust-Building Behaviors

Your partner lied to you. He concealed things from you. There were things going on inside him that he did not tell you about and there was a relationship with another woman that he hid from you.

Now he wants you to believe that that is all in the past, that he won't ever do those things again, that you can trust him again. But how can you? You need proof, and lots of it, and you don't yet have that assurance. There's only one way to get it: by him showing you, through his actions, over and over again, that he's now being open and honest with you.

So how does he do this? Well, you have to tell him how. You have to tell him what you want to see from him. In her book *After the Affair*, Janis Abrahms Spring (1996) does an excellent job of instructing a couple on how to do this. She talks about making a list of trust-building behaviors that are meaningful to you; actions he can take that are reassuring and that demonstrate that he is doing whatever he can to act in a trustworthy manner. Some of these behaviors ask more from your partner than others. Spring divides the list into low-cost behaviors and high-cost behaviors. An example she gives of the former is "Limit your overnight travel" (p. 149), and an example of the latter is "Don't contact or associate with your lover's circle of friends or relatives" (p. 156). We recommend this book as an excellent resource to help you in rebuilding the trust.

As you're working with your partner on your personal list of trust-building behaviors, remember that what you ask him to do has to be realistic and respectful. Part of you probably wants to put him in a box so there is no chance that he could ever betray you. Part of you wants to tell him to never look or speak to anyone of the opposite sex again. But if you are ever going to be able to trust him again in the real world, you have to let him have a real life, with all its attendant distractions and temptations that he does not give in to.

Should You Ever Trust Him Again?

In the end, your partner can only do so much to regain your trust. He can be there through the tough discussions, help you work through your pain and rage, be understanding, and express his regret. He can work with you on making a list of trust-building behaviors and then follow through and do all of those things, again and again.

At some point, though, you're going to have to choose to take the risk of really trusting him again. That means letting go of your anger. It means not letting your fear of being heartbroken again control you. It means really letting him into your heart again, not protecting yourself by keeping him at arm's length. It means believing him when he tells you something and not checking up on him.

This is a scary choice to make, but of course it's the only one if you want to be happy with him again. If you fearfully refuse to trust him again even after he's done everything he can over a significant period of time (at least a number of months), you're putting your LTLR in danger just as surely as he did by being unfaithful. Then it's your problem, not his. You can't allow your fear to sabotage you and the relationship in this way.

Can you be certain that he won't betray you again? No, of course not. But review how hard he has worked to earn back your trust. If you can't come up with concrete reasons for why he doesn't deserve to be trusted again, make the leap. It's the only way you'll be able to find happiness in love again, for if you can't make this leap of faith, it's unlikely that you'll be able to do so with any other man in the future.

A Final Thought for the Partner Who Strayed

One of the most common things that happens as a couple is working through the aftermath of an infidelity is that the partner who was unfaithful gets impatient. He becomes exasperated that he's been doing everything his partner has asked of him and she still doesn't trust him. Unfortunately, the sad truth of the matter is that the wound caused by your betrayal is so deep that it does take a long time to heal.

You may be truly committed to her. You may have learned your lesson, grown, and matured. There may be absolutely no chance that you would ever be unfaithful and risk your relationship again. But think of it from her point of view; you're asking her to again trust you with her heart after you've just stomped on it. That's asking a lot. So when you feel frustrated and impatient with her failure to believe in you, remember, she has a right to be cautious.

YOUR PARTNERS IN HEALING AND THEIR EFFORTS

The process of regaining trust and rebuilding your love and intimacy after an infidelity differs for all couples. But reading about how our four couples have continued to navigate their way through that journey can help you do the same in your LTLR.

■ Gracie and Jake: An Infidelity of Fear

In order to deal with her Infidelity of Fear, Gracie had to push herself to discover the source of the fear that led her to be unfaithful. She also had to uncover how she was able to convince herself that having infidelities was a solution to her unhappiness and sense of frustration. It was a challenge for her, as it is for every betraying partner, to remain open to hearing about the pain, fear, and rage her actions caused in her partner. Jake, for his part, had to push himself to be honest about his feelings, especially his anger, and stay in the difficult discussions with Gracie. This couple desperately needed to learn that their pattern of Conflict Avoidance aggravated their difficulties and stymied effective resolutions in their relationship.

After six months and much perseverance, hard work, and pain, Gracie and Jake were able to identify their personal fears and limitations and gain confidence that they were standing on solid ground in their relationship. Gracie struggled with her angry and dissatisfied feelings. She fought recognizing her fears about being overlooked, fears that had fueled her flight into infidelity. Jake was able to acknowledge how he had selectively ignored his intuitions and avoided conflict in the relationship. As a result, both started feeling that they had begun to construct a more stable relationship by developing and using the tools of Self-Intimacy and Conflict Intimacy. They could see their success in working through hurt, blame, and shame, as well as the rebuilding of trust in the relationship and in one another. Their feelings of love for one another began to reawaken.

■ Samantha and Paul:
An Infidelity of Loneliness

Though he had his doubts about whether it would work, Paul decided that he wanted to make a go at seeing if he and Samantha could rekindle their relationship after his affair. For her part, Samantha was torn between feeling desperate to have a second chance with Paul and wanting to punish him for devastating her. She also found it very difficult to believe that Paul was no longer seeing Mary or at least not thinking about her and missing her. It took Samantha a few months before she was ready to let go of her anger and desire to punish Paul and become ready to talk about her underlying hurt.

After a couple more months, she was willing to hear about how much Paul missed Mary. This was quite a struggle for Samantha, but by assuming the role of the Inquirer, she challenged herself to hear Paul's experience and not take his feelings personally. Eventually she was able to hear how lonely Paul had felt and how she had been previously unable to understand and acknowledge his feelings. Samantha also realized that she too had been shut down in the relationship and came to appreciate how she had contributed to the relationship's difficulties and limitations.

As Samantha was able to listen to Paul's loneliness, he found himself able to acknowledge how his dissatisfaction had grown over time without his awareness and how his emotional limitations had led him to become vulnerable to infidelity. As Paul became more practiced at being conflict intimate with Samantha, he was able to share his feelings with her rather than stuffing or minimizing them and risking that they again hijack his commitment to his marriage.

■ Amy and Lewis:
An Infidelity of Anger

Of our three couples struggling with infidelity, Amy and Lewis have an especially difficult path back to intimacy. Amy stayed wedded to her outrage and the devastation at learning of Lewis's many infidelities. She vacillated between anger and blame and the fear of losing him. She felt lost in the confusion of her feelings for a couple of months.

Lewis struggled for just as long not to retreat to his familiar anger and the distortion that he was justified in his behaviors. He found it particularly difficult to listen to Amy's feelings of hurt. He kept taking them personally and hearing them as criticism and revenge rather than pain and fear. He had to resist arguing that his actions were justified and pointing out his view of Amy's part in the problems. But after a couple of months he found himself able to stop reacting and really listen. This then allowed him to squarely face the limited and unsuccessful ways he had dealt with his feelings of hurt, disappointment, and anger. As he acknowledged how emotionally unequipped he had been to see a relationship as only great or awful, he could also admit how vulnerable he had felt in their relationship and express these feelings in a more constructive rather than defensive way.

As Amy healed from the heartbreak of the betrayals, she examined why she had accepted so little in the relationship and acknowledged how her own fears of a man's anger and/or disapproval had limited her ability to be a more capable partner. Consequently she found more emotionally mature ways to stand up for herself in the face of Lewis's disapproval and disagreement and learned to accept that agreement is not necessary, but mutual respect is.

It took about twelve months of concerted work marked by both progress and setbacks before Amy and Lewis started feeling a glimmer of confidence that they could each heal from the past. They began to see that they could base their relationship more on mutual love and respect and less on self-protection or the fear of loss.

Today Amy and Lewis describe their relationship as a work in progress. The growth of the relationship invigorates them and has begun to replace the excitement of their old passionate ups and downs. They're now able to have faith in their individual and mutual abilities to stay committed to Self-Intimacy and Conflict Intimacy.

Chapter Review

Making Your Relationship Infidelity Proof
No matter which type of infidelity your partner had, the way to get from infidelity to intimacy is a two-part process:

1. You will have to work through the deep hurt, disappointment, rage, and other negative feelings. You can accomplish this by using the ESA exercise and the I-to-I exercise.

2. After you are both more capable of being self-intimate and conflict intimate, your efforts then will go into rebuilding your ability to trust your partner again. You can start to do this by making a list of trust-building behaviors and then sharing these with your partner.

Reminders and Cautions
Healing your relationship requires both understanding its foundation—the levels of SI, CI, and AI—as well as a clear understanding of how the infidelity was born. For most couples this process takes nine to eighteen months of concerted effort. By working on and understanding these two things, the two of you will be creating an infidelity-resistant relationship.

Are you both committed to continuing to remain open and honest with one another as the relationship improves? Many couples risk becoming complacent again once the worst pain has passed. This would be a mistake and would put your relationship at great risk again. A relationship is a garden that requires constant weeding and feeding.

chapter 13

loving with security: making your relationship infidelity-safe

We enjoy warmth because we have been cold.
We appreciate light because we have been in
darkness. By the same token, we can experience
joy because we have known sadness.
—David Weatherford

Getting to the place where you never have to worry about your partner being unfaithful again is what this book is all about. Our many years of working with couples whose Long-Term Love Relationships have been shattered by infidelity has taught us that there is only one way to get there: the two of you respond to the infidelity by building an LTLR that is so strong and healthy in its intimacy, so filled with love and joy in being together, that neither of you would ever consider wanting to be with another person. The secret to achieving this lies in understanding that your love for each other is totally dependent upon the vibrancy of your emotional intimacy.

Once the initial honeymoon phase (Sweet Symbiosis) of a Long-Term Love Relationship ends, the fuel that will power you forward is emotional intimacy. Without it, love fails and the LTLR crashes and burns.

As soon as either of you allows the openness with which you share your emotions to diminish, the bond of your love is weakened. Conversely, the most powerful way to strengthen that bond of love is to enhance the honesty, empathy, and respect in your emotional communications, especially when you're in conflict.

Establish a history of dealing with conflict well together and your love for each other will deepen. Not only that, you'll start building a sense of security in the relationship; you'll sense that the two of you can get through anything. With such a strong LTLR foundation, the seeds of infidelity cannot take root. That is because fear, loneliness, and anger—feelings that when left unattended to will lead to infidelity—get brought up early, before they have a chance to grow in strength. As these emotions get discussed and dealt with, they lose the power to shatter your relationship through infidelity.

That emotional intimacy is what a healthy Long-Term Love Relationship is all about. Your partner's betrayal has demonstrated in an excruciating way that your relationship didn't have it. But if you both want it, if you both are committed to doing the necessary work, you can have it. The building blocks of such a relationship are the three intimacies. Build those into your LTLR, and the three infidelities will never threaten your love again. In this final chapter, we'll teach you how to take full advantage of the three intimacies, and we'll give you some customized instructions based on which of the three infidelities your partner engaged in.

THE FIRST STEPS: GETTING PAST SOURED SYMBIOSIS

As we revealed in chapter 3, infidelities happen when a couple is stuck in stage 2 of the LTLR developmental process, Soured Symbiosis. This halt in progress can happen in two ways. First, after going through stage 1, Sweet Symbiosis, an LTLR can get arrested at stage 2 because the couple doesn't have the tools necessary to deal with their differences and conflicts. They can remain in stage 2 for years, even decades, if they don't acquire those intimacy tools. The longer they wallow in stage 2, the more dissatisfying, unfulfilling, and unhappy their LTLR will become. Feelings of fear, loneliness, or anger will grow and often lead to an infidelity.

The second way a couple gets stuck at stage 2 is by regressing back to it because of a great stress or trauma, such as the loss of a job, a disabling injury, the death of a child, or a serious illness. In response to such a stress or multiple such stressors, a couple that had previously moved past Soured Symbiosis may revert to stage 2's less mature functioning. Fear, loneliness, or anger start building up, aren't dealt with, and again frequently lead to an infidelity.

The Three Intimacies: The Key to Getting Out of the Danger Zone

Whichever way you and your partner got into Soured Symbiosis, your task now is to work your way out of it. Failure to do so is the surest way to never fully heal from the trauma of the infidelity, and the surest way to set your LTLR up for another one.

Stage 2 is the infidelity danger zone, and there is but one way out of it: developing high levels of the three intimacies in your relationship. Do that and your LTLR will move forward to the safety zones of stages 3 and 4. In these stages, the emotions that drive a partner into an infidelity are never allowed to build up and acquire the power that leads to betrayal.

Sure, fear, loneliness, and anger are still felt at times in stages 3 and 4, but because of your highly developed Self-Intimacy and Conflict Intimacy, you're aware of them when they arise and you and your partner talk about and work through them. Your awareness of these feelings and you and your partner's ability to deal with them openly and respectfully brings you two closer together, cements your bond, and deepens your love.

So the first steps to making sure that your partner never engages in another infidelity are the development of true Self-Intimacy, Conflict Intimacy, and Affection Intimacy.

In working on the three intimacies, you and your partner both want to focus most directly on your capacity for Self-Intimacy, and then on together building your Conflict Intimacy. This will power the growth of your Affection Intimacy. That is, with heightened Self-Intimacy and Conflict Intimacy, you both will find yourselves starting to feel loving again and wanting to express that love verbally and through your actions and sexuality.

As was detailed in the chapters on the three types of infidelity, being able to identify which one of the three infidelity types your partner engaged in gives you vital information about which of the three intimacies you and he most need to work on. Instead of just being a passive victim of the betrayal, making good use of this insight enables you to become stronger in your ability to take care of yourself and make your LTLR healthy, loving, and safe.

This could mean that your partner gets himself into therapy to work on his Self-Intimacy and his deep-seated fear that led him to have an Infidelity of Fear. It could mean the two of you working on your Self-Intimacy so that you become more adept at sharing your inner selves with each other since the failure to do this and the failure to then develop Conflict Intimacy led him to have an Infidelity of Loneliness. Or it could mean that your partner needs to address his issues with anger and the two of you have to work hard to develop Conflict Intimacy, dissipating built-up anger and removing any reason to have another Infidelity of Anger.

As hard as it is to hear, you can extract something positive out of the agony of his betrayal. In fact, you *must* do so if you hope to really heal and rebuild your LTLR so that it is healthy enough to last. Getting the relationship past Soured Symbiosis is the key to accomplishing this. The secret to being able to do that is to learn what three intimacy weaknesses exist both within your relationship and within you and your partner, and you get this information from recognizing what type of infidelity he had. Once you've learned from this analysis, then it's all about you and your partner being willing to do the work necessary to propel your

LTLR out of Soured Symbiosis and into the fulfillment and safety of Differentiation and Synergy.

BECOMING INVULNERABLE TO AN INFIDELITY OF FEAR

Of the three types of infidelity, making your Long-Term Love Relationship invulnerable to future Infidelities of Fear depends on you, the betrayed partner, the least. While you can definitely help create the necessary changes, avoiding another infidelity is much more about your partner's relationship with himself, his Self-Intimacy, than it is about his relationship with you.

Your partner has to start by identifying and acknowledging the deep fear (of intimacy, commitment, or being unworthy of love) that is driving him. Then he has to work through it and unmask the false beliefs about himself and about love relationships that it is based on. The goal is to replace these beliefs with healthier ones. His fear will never completely disappear, but that's okay. By confronting and wrestling with it, he will become stronger and his fear will become weaker. If he has enough courage to do this work, his fear will lose the strength to control him; it will no longer have the power to drive him to betray you.

Because this is a real challenge for anyone to accomplish, we recommend that your partner go into individual counseling specifically to work through his fear. Doing so demonstrates that he is taking this seriously and is really committed to doing the work necessary to make certain he never betrays you again.

You can help him in this process. In fact, he needs to let you help him. But you can only do so if he talks with you about his fear. He will be increasing his Self-Intimacy so that he is aware of his fear when it arises and can identify what is causing it. Then he needs to talk with you about these things.

That's where Conflict Intimacy comes in. You need to be able to listen to what's going on with him and not get defensive, not let your own fear or your anger get in the way of helping him. You need him to see that your relationship is a safe place for him to be open and honest with these feelings that make him feel weak and vulnerable. In this way, you can help him to overcome them. In this way, his fear is dealt with constructively and strengthens your relationship.

If he does not open up with you about his fear, this is a sure sign that he is not really confronting it, a sure sign that your LTLR is still in danger.

BECOMING INVULNERABLE TO AN INFIDELITY OF LONELINESS

As with any of the three types of infidelities, the first step in making your LTLR invulnerable to an Infidelity of Loneliness reoccurring in the future is truly healing from this betrayal. As we discussed in detail in chapter 1, this involves working through your terrible pain, anger, and fear as well as your partner earning your trust back over time.

At the same time, you and your partner have to address head-on the two factors that led to his betrayal. First is his low Self-Intimacy, which allowed his loneliness to grow unchecked so that it came to overtake and control him, leading to the infidelity. Your partner absolutely must commit to work on building up his SI, not only so that he becomes highly aware of the emotions he is feeling, but also so that he is then able to talk with you about them, whether good or bad. If he does not do this, another Infidelity of Loneliness will likely occur in the future.

Second, you and he have to address the low Conflict Intimacy that led to the distance between you. This is what gave birth to the loneliness that enabled his infidelity.

Either through the Conflict Avoidant or Hostile Dependent style of dealing with your differences, you and your partner have consistently failed to successfully resolve your conflicts. Hurt, disappointment, anger, and other negative feelings have therefore built up inside each of you. Those feelings have become like a wall between you. Where early in your LTLR there was warmth and closeness, now there is iciness and distance. You're both starving for love and your love is starved. No wonder loneliness has thrived in this bitter landscape.

Building Conflict Intimacy is the only way to bring love into your LTLR again. It's the only way to break down the wall of negative emotions that separates you. These negative feelings have to be dealt with in order for you to heal your relationship and become close, intimate, and loving again. By developing the ability to be intimate in conflict, you will rediscover the desire to be intimate in love.

BECOMING INVULNERABLE TO AN INFIDELITY OF ANGER

Much like with an Infidelity of Loneliness, after doing the difficult work to heal from the pain and trauma of the betrayal, the keys to making sure this never happens again center around your partner overcoming his low Self-Intimacy and the two of you developing your Conflict Intimacy.

Your partner must commit to work on growing his Self-Intimacy, especially in regard to how he handles hurt and disappointment, the two emotions that underlie and fuel his anger. He must develop his in-the-moment awareness of these emotions and then practice talking with you constructively, in a non-blaming way, about them.

In addition, he must do the hard work necessary to identify and work through the pain and anger he has built up from his past. He absolutely must own that the roots of the anger that led to his infidelity predate his relationship with you. And it's not only about the mistreatment and abuse he suffered at the hands of others that led to his problem with anger. It's also about how he's never dealt with his anger effectively.

By building his Self-Intimacy, he will learn how to constructively deal with his anger and the hurts and disappointments that lead to it. Only then will he be able to work through his anger from the past. Only after this will he be safe from being hijacked by his anger in the future. And only then will the danger of his anger controlling him, causing him to act out for revenge, be eliminated. Individual counseling is an important consideration for him as he is likely to have difficulty putting aside his feeling that his infidelity was justified, and he may struggle to listen to you express your pain and anger.

Next, you and he together have to work on developing the Conflict Intimacy in your relationship. You cannot afford to continue dealing with conflict in either the Hostile Dependent or the Conflict Avoidant style. You both have to learn to solve your differences as a team, not approaching them in an attacking, defensive way and not brushing them under the rug. You must deal with conflict openly and constructively, with each of you taking responsibility for your part in the problems and each of you expressing caring and regret for the pain you have caused your partner.

When you both have done these things, anger will no longer have the power to hijack your Long-Term Love Relationship by causing an Infidelity of Anger.

YOU CAN GO HOME AGAIN

Throughout this book we've talked about the building blocks of healthy Long-Term Love Relationships, using a building as a metaphor. When they're working well, LTLRs are like a warm (sometimes hot!), cozy home, a sanctuary that is inviting and safe.

When an infidelity occurs, that sanctuary disappears, the walls of the structure crumble. This book is all about rebuilding, constructing together a new home that is stronger than the old one, built to last forever. We've given you the building blocks that empower you to do this in your LTLR. We've worked with countless couples who have used them to do just that.

But what we can't give you is the strength necessary to take the risk of giving your partner a second chance. Sometimes he doesn't deserve one. But if he is willing to do the necessary work, we hope that you find the courage to build anew with him. For then your love can come back. Then you can create an LTLR that fulfills you for the rest of your life. Then you can go home again.

■ Cindy and Scott:
Growing Pains Without Infidelity

Cindy and Scott's path through ten-plus years of marriage was no easier than the challenges our other three couples faced. So how is it that neither of them chose an infidelity? What did they have going for them? How did they stay out of the danger zone?

They had three key elements: sufficient Self-Intimacy, a commitment to Conflict Intimacy, and a willingness to recognize and repair their contribution to the relationship problems. While they did seek marital counseling as both felt stuck in their old conflicts, neither was motivated by strong feelings of loneliness, anger, or fear. And each had sufficient Self-Intimacy to enable them to seek more for themselves and the relationship. With assistance, each was able to better identify and express both their negative and positive feelings about their marriage. And as a result, they were able to listen and come to respect rather than argue or retreat from their partner's feelings and concerns. Their developing commitment to Conflict Intimacy meant that each was willing to stay in the disagreements and not avoid or escalate them.

In spite of Cindy's disappointment with Scott's unwillingness to share his feelings and air out their grievances, she never chose to cross the fidelity boundary because she viewed her feelings as a realistic appraisal of her situation, and she was unwilling to sacrifice the integrity of her commitment to Scott and herself for her frustrations. Instead, she persevered in her efforts to talk with Scott about how her growing disappointments were affecting her feelings for him.

To his credit, Scott worked hard to listen to Cindy's feelings and overcome hearing them as threats. Instead, he reminded himself that she was sharing what was true for her and he believed that she was earnest. Scott's Self-Intimacy was great enough for him to stay in touch with his feelings, both positive and negative. He also was willing to share these with Cindy.

As the two of them continued to chip away at their differences and disappointments, they eventually found themselves able to appreciate the other's needs and concerns without feeling that they were in competition. This was not an easy route. From time to time, each would regress to insisting that the other give in. But their persistence paid off as they found themselves slowly but surely progressing from Soured Symbiosis to Differentiation and Synergy.

Scott and Cindy sought counseling for help in getting past some of their most entrenched problems. Cindy specifically needed to work on her belief that she asked for very little but gave a lot, and that therefore, when she asked for something, she was justified in expecting compliance. By pushing herself to remain self-intimate and talk about her feelings and assumptions in the I-to-I format, she came to view their conflicts about requests and responses in a different light. She no longer viewed noncompliance as stubbornness but rather as a choice and the expression of Scott's preferences.

Scott needed to work on his fear of Cindy's disapproval and his belief that she should know he was a good guy and not express criticism of him. By working on his Self-Intimacy and admitting his fear and discomfort with disapproval, Scott was able to respect Cindy's negative feelings as expressions of who she was and realize that he did not need to change or take her feelings as a comment about him.

Consequently, Cindy and Scott found a path toward greater faith and confidence in their relationship. Out of this, their Affection Intimacy grew and reminded them of why they had originally been attracted to one another.

Lastly, no matter how frustrated, disappointed, and angry Cindy and Scott became, each was unwilling to avoid and ignore their problems. Neither could live with the dissatisfaction present in the relationship; they knew that things could be better and were unwilling to settle for something less. Their commitment to themselves and the relationship laid the foundation for each taking responsibility for their part in their struggles and growth.

FINAL THOUGHTS

You and your partner have been through the worst. Your life together has been shaken to its foundation, but all is not lost. We opened this chapter with a quotation talking about being able to appreciate joy because we have known sadness. While this may seem trite, it is true. You have known the depths of despair and we assure you that you can come back from this to find hope, love, and security.

Many couples who have done the hard work to recover from an infidelity and rebuild their relationship have told us that while the infidelity was the lowest point in their life, it also eventually led them to a level of intimacy, happiness, and commitment that they only dared dream might exist. Although they are emphatic that the way their partner went about "informing" them of his unhappiness in their LTLR was both devastating and wrong, they also admit that maybe such a traumatic means was the wake-up call both of them needed in order to address the ruptures in their relationship.

Now you have the tools to get through the betrayal as well as deepen and strengthen your Long-Term Love Relationship. Use these tools and we guarantee that each of you will become excellent LTLR partners, making each other feel so loved and happy that neither of you will ever want to be with anyone else.

You have experienced the cold, the darkness, and the sadness; do this work together and you will bask in warmth, light, and joy.

Chapter Review

You can go home again. And this requires that each of you commit to the following five goals:

1. Getting past Soured Symbiosis.

2. Continuing to practice the three intimacies—the key to getting out of the danger zone.

3. Being expert at emotional self-awareness as one of the most potent means to avoid feelings of fear, loneliness, or anger.

4. Staying focused on feelings that suggest that you may be vulnerable to infidelity, paying specific attention to the emotions leading to the three infidelities.

5. And lastly, gaining and maintaining perspective on the dark sides of intimacy and respecting that it indicates growth and a need for attention rather than avoidance. By doing so, you can appreciate the light side of passion, especially as you and your partner have each had a hand in creating and maintaining it.

appendix a

the emotional self-awareness (ESA) exercise

The primary way for you to develop Self-Intimacy is by practicing the Emotional Self-Awareness (ESA) Exercise. Ask yourself the following three questions two to three times a day:

1. What emotion(s) am I feeling right now?

2. What situation or perception of mine is causing me to feel this emotion(s)?

3. What, if anything, can I do about this causal situation to take good care of myself?

ESA Exercise Points to Remember

- Refocusing in this structured way from the external world onto your internal world is all that is needed for profound growth in Self-Intimacy.

- The ESA exercise is the most effective when it is done on an ongoing, day-by-day basis. If you do it for ninety consecutive days, you will see the most change in your Self-Intimacy.

- Do the exercise for just two to three minutes each time for the best results.

- Share your ESA exercise insights with your partner, best friends, and family. This is a way of becoming more self-intimate and of defining yourself, of differentiating.

Common Problems in Performing the ESA Exercise

- Failure to remember to do it: a mnemonic (memory) device is often needed (for example, tying it to every time you go to the bathroom). Not remembering to do it can be a symptom of lack of motivation.

- The inability to get in touch with emotions or know what they are (this is especially common for men). Use a list of feelings (see appendix D) to help you determine what emotion(s) you are feeling and remember that if you keep trying, you will be able to gain access and know what the feeling is; practice is all it takes.

- Remember, working on the ESA exercise is vital since Self-Intimacy is a key to relationship development; without it, significant restrictions on intimacy with your partner exist.

appendix b

the initiator-inquirer (I-to-I) exercise guidelines

The primary way for you to develop conflict intimacy is by practicing the Initiator-Inquirer Exercise (I-to-I). A review of the two roles follows.

Reminders for the Initiator

1. Talk about you.

2. Focus on one issue only and be specific.

3. Pick an issue that you are afraid to share.

4. Structure your sharing around "I feel x because of y."

5. Don't blame your partner; remember, this is about you.

6. Your goal is to help your partner know your reality.

Reminders for the Inquirer

1. Fight getting defensive; keep reminding yourself
    that what your partner shares is about him or her,
    not about you.

2. Recap.

3. Be curious; your task is to "step in their
    moccasins."

4. Ask questions to help you understand your partner;
    don't ask questions designed to defend yourself.

5. Don't problem solve.

appendix c

the I-to-I maturity goals handouts

After you have had some practice as the Initiator, please review this diagram.
Locate place(s) where you see yourself. Then, on the Goals page attached, decide what next steps
you want to work on as you continue to practice the "i-to-i" process with your partner.

" ....When something is bothering me..."

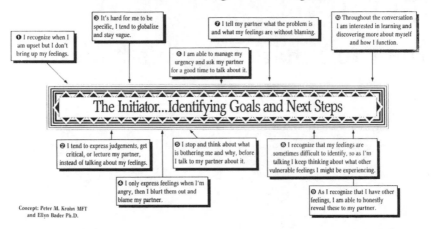

After you have had some practice as the Inquirer, please review this diagram.
Locate place(s) where you see yourself. Then, on the Goals page attached, decide what next steps
you want to work on as you continue to practice the "i-to-i" process with your partner.

" ....When my partner is upset and talks to me..."

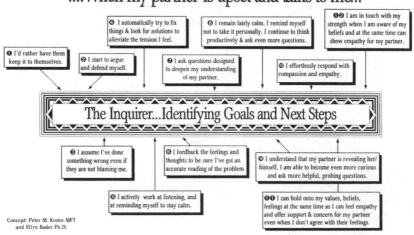

appendix d

a brief list of emotions

Abandoned	Disgusted	Jealous
Adoring	Ecstatic	Lonely
Afraid	Embarrassed	Love Struck
Angry	Enraged	Lustful
Anxious	Excited	Mischievous
Appreciative	Exhausted	Needy
Ashamed	Fearful	Sad
Awed	Frightened	Safe
Bereft	Frustrated	Selfish
Bored	Furious	Shocked
Cautious	Greedy	Shy
Confident	Guilty	Smug
Confused	Happy	Suspicious
Depressed	Hatred	Touched
Desperate	Hopeful	Trusting
Disappointed	Irate	Vindictive

resources

The Good Divorce: Keeping Your Family Together When Your Marriage Comes Apart. By Constance Ahrons.   If you determine that your relationship is unsalvageable, this is a fine resource for making the best of a very sad choice. It is an especially important book if you have children.

Tell Me No Lies: How to Face the Truth and Build a Loving Marriage. By Ellyn Bader and Peter T. Pearson.   Written by two psychologists who specialize in marriages and relationships, the book focuses on how we inadvertently or deliberately lie to our partners to avoid conflict. The authors bring their own marriage to the text as well as sample couples who illustrate the choices couples make that result in strengthening or weakening relationships and intimacy.

Around the House and in the Garden: A Memoir of Heartbreak, Healing, and Home Improvement. By Dominique Browning.   A good book to read as you're recovering from an infidelity alone or when you're choosing a divorce. Browning provides hope that you will recover and rediscover yourself.

Back from Betrayal: Saving a Marriage, a Family, a Life. By Suzy Farbman. Afterword by Burton Farbman.   This book is written by a woman who discovered her husband's infidelity after twenty-five years of marriage. She does an excellent job of communicating her devastation and sense of disorientation. The book includes the details of her recovery from the hurt and her personal work to heal in therapy. A wonderful addition to the book is the afterword by her husband, who writes honestly and frankly about his infidelities, his reasoning, and his reckoning with his choices, and their effects on his wife, himself, and their marriage. This is an excellent book to read once you have gotten past the initial shock of the discovery.

If the Buddha Married: Creating Enduring Relationships on a Spiritual Path. By Charlotte Kasl.   This book offers practical and sound guidance to remind the reader of what contributes to a strong, loving, and growing partnership. It's a great primer on marriage.

Letting Go of Anger: The 10 Most Common Anger Styles and What to Do About Them. By Ron Potter-Efron and Pat Potter-Efron.   Both authors are family therapists and offer a simple and elegant description of the ways most of us express anger immaturely. The book also provides a clear description of what mature and responsible anger looks and sounds like. This is an excellent book that we recommend to most of our clients.

After the Affair: Healing the Pain and Rebuilding Trust When a Partner Has Been Unfaithful. By Janis Abrahms Spring.   Janis Spring is a clinical psychologist who specializes in helping couples overcome infidelities. Her book is a salve for those who are suffering from the discovery of betrayal and is equally as profound for the unfaithful partner. She does a fine job of describing what each partner is going through. She also presents the reader with checklists and practical ways to negotiate rebuilding trust.

How Can I Forgive You? The Courage to Forgive, the Freedom Not To. By Abrahms Spring.   This book is for all readers who struggle with knowing how to forgive a betraying partner—or anyone who has violated your relationship. Retribution and revenge are discussed in depth and two healthier alternatives are provided: acceptance and genuine forgiveness. The author defines acceptance as a means of self-care when the offender won't or can't assist in the healing process. Genuine forgiveness is the result of the work of both people as the offender earns forgiveness while the hurt party takes action to grant forgiveness. Steps to accomplish both acceptance and genuine forgiveness are provided.

Surviving Infidelity: Making Decisions, Recovering from the Pain. By Rona Subotnik and Gloria Harris.   This is a nuts-and-bolts approach to making the decision to stay or go. It offers a range of considerations and helps the reader with specific ways to deal with obsessive thoughts and many fears and feelings.

Straight talk About Betrayal: A Self-Help Guide for Couples. By Donna R. Bellafiore.   This small book is a powerhouse of information about the stages of emotional responses that couples go through with any significant betrayal. The author provides the reader with simple, clear and powerful information and a guide for how to work their way out of the haze that a betrayal brings to a relationship. The reader is empowered with steps to help them maintain stability and how to determine if the partners want to recover and rebuild the relationship.

My Husband's Affair became the BEST thing that ever happened to me. By Anne Bercht   This book is written for the reader who is in the throes of a partner's betrayal and needs encouragement to know she's neither crazy nor alone in her agony AND that she will survive the pain and devastation. The author is frank and open about her own odyssey through the betrayal and provides the reader with exacting details about how the awfulness of the discovery later became the opening for a new and better relationship with her husband. Her husband and daughter also write about their pain and learning.

references

Bader, Ellyn, and Peter Krohn. 1996. Maturity Goals Handout.

Bader, Ellyn, and Peter Pearson. 1988. *In Quest of the Mythical Mate: A Developmental Approach to Diagnosis and Treatment in Couples Therapy*. New York: Routledge.

———. 2000. *Tell Me No Lies: How to Face the Truth and Build a Loving Marriage*. New York: Golden Books.

Brown, Emily. 2001. *Patterns of Infidelity and Their Treatment*. Philadelphia: Brunner-Routledge.

Glass, Shirley. 2003. *Not "Just Friends": Rebuilding Trust and Recovering Your Sanity After Infidelity*. New York: Free Press.

Lusterman, Don-David. 1998. *Infidelity: A Survival Guide*. Oakland, CA: New Harbinger Publications.

Maslow, Abraham. 1968. *Toward a Psychology of Being*. New York: Van Nostrand Reinhold Company.

The Random House Dictionary of the English Language. 1987. New York: Random House.

Spring, Janis Abrahms. 1996. *After the Affair: Healing the Pain and Rebuilding Trust When a Partner Has Been Unfaithful*. New York: HarperCollins.

Vaughan, Peggy. 1998. *The Monogamy Myth*. New York: Newmarket Press.

Steven D. Solomon, Ph.D., is a licensed clinical psychologist who specializes in couples therapy. He has been in private practice in La Jolla, CA, for more than twenty years. He is a founding director of the Relationship Institute and past president of the San Diego Psychological Association, the United Jewish Federation of San Diego County, and Hillel of San Diego. He and his wife, Esther, have been married for twenty-one years and are the very proud parents of their son, Lewis.

Lorie J. Teagno, Ph.D., is a licensed clinical psychologist in La Jolla, CA, where she has worked in private practice for more than twenty years. A founding director of The Relationship Institute, she has been an adjunct lecturer at United States International University. She has provided training for many therapists in couples counseling.

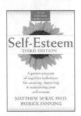